J. M. J.

Thoughts and Counsels
for
Women of the World.

By MGR. LE COURTIER,
BISHOP OF MONTPELLIER.

FROM THE FRENCH
By MARIE CLOTILDE REDFERN.

Catholic Authors Press
www.CatholicAuthors.com

TO MY MOTHER

I DEDICATE THIS TRANSLATION

WITH DEEPEST DEVOTION.

Copyright 1895 Clotilde Redfern
2007 Catholic Authors Press

ISBN: 978-0-9782985-0-0

Catholic Authors Press

Hartford, Connecticut

www.CatholicAuthors.org

LETTER OF APPROBATION FROM HIS EMINENCE
THE LATE CARDINAL ARCHBISHOP OF PARIS.

We authorize the printing and publication in our diocese of the work entitled : *"Thoughts and Counsels for Women of the World" (Annual Retreat for Ladies), preached in the Cathedral of Paris from 1849 to 1860, by Mgr. Le Courtier, Canon, Theologian and Pastor of that Church,* and we recommend this substantial book to those for whom it is designed. They will find united in it, in the form of *souvenirs and simple notes* as the author modestly calls them, rules of conduct on the great principles of the christian life, traced by a sure hand ; observations and details of customs, the fruit of a long experience and deep knowledge of the world, which cannot fail to inspire the most salutary reflections.

✠ F. N. CARDINAL MORLOT,
Archbishop of Paris.

PARIS, *March 14th*, 1860.

LETTER OF APPROBATION FROM HIS EMINENCE
THE CARDINAL ARCHBISHOP OF BALTIMORE.

We approve of the publication of the Work, entitled: "*Thoughts and Counsels for Women of the World,*" *translated from the French of Mgr. Le Courtier, Bishop of Montpellier*, and we cordially unite with the Episcopacy of France in recommending it as a Work calculated to promote piety and devotion among the pious faithful.

The translation is easy and graceful, and deserving of encouragement, that others may be induced to spend their leisure moments in similar good works.

A free circulation of the Work in our Archdiocese, will meet our heartfelt approbation.

✠ J. CARD. GIBBONS,
Archbishop of Baltimore.

ARCHIEPISCOPAL RESIDENCE,
April 10*th*, 1895.

LETTER FROM THE VERY REVEREND PROVINCIAL OF THE JESUITS OF THE NEW YORK AND MARYLAND PROVINCE.

At a period when so much is being said and written about woman, and woman's rights, and when woman's so-called "sphere" is being enlarged to such an extent as to destroy her real power in her true sphere, "Thoughts and Counsels for Women of the World" becomes a most valuable book for the times.

Its clear and pointed lessons couched in language just as clear and just as pointed, will furnish abundant food for thought, not only in time of "retreat," but every day in the year.

Those especially who glory in the title of Children of Mary, the world over, will learn from this book to know more about their Mother and their Model so beautifully called by the Holy Spirit in the book of Genesis: *The Woman.*

W. O'B. PARDOW, S. J.

COLLEGE OF ST. FRANCIS XAVIER,
 NEW YORK, *September* 2, 1895.

TRANSLATOR'S PREFACE.

Thinking these discourses most practical, and that they would fill a need in this country, I have ventured, in spite of my inexperience, to translate and publish them; hoping with the author that they may accomplish much good, while I trust that I have been faithful in giving his spirit and his style. The date of the lectures must be considered in some few instances. There are also some points which apply to French customs and not our own.

M. C. R.

INTRODUCTION.

We are not giving the faithful carefully written conferences; our occupations would not permit this considerable work.

We offer to those who followed us during twelve years some *souvenirs, simple notes* which will enable them to recall what they have heard.

We hope that this work, which is scarcely roughhewn, will give the basis of the instruction sufficiently, and that the chisel of meditation, examining and searching deeper, will soften the inequalities, the rude imperfections of style.

Those who wish some *souvenirs* urge us to publish these *notes*. We give them as we can, being more desirous of doing good than of assuring our reputation, praying the Lord to add growth and maturity to this coarse cultivation, to this very imperfect sprinkling.

Le Courtier,
Canon-Pastor.

CONTENTS.

	PAGE.
Inutility of the Retreat,	9
The Abuse of Graces,	25
The Love of God,	36
The Flight of the Love of the World,	52
The Pleasures of the World,	68
Duties of the Rich,	75
Portrait of the Christian Woman,	101
The Regulated Life,	120
Woman's Sunday,	133
The Useful Life,	149
Woman's Conversation,	160
The Life of Union with God,	178
The Exercise of Prayer and Meditation,	189
The Life of Self-Denial,	202
The Christian Mission of Women,	216

ANNUAL RETREAT FOR LADIES.

INUTILITY OF THE RETREAT.

> *Ibi loquar ad cor ejus.*
> "There I will speak to her heart."
> Osee, II, 14

NECESSITY of the retreat, utility of the retreat, means of profiting by it, fruits that it should produce—this, Ladies, is the happy and almost invariable theme that opens and consecrates the spiritual exercises which we are commencing to-day.

This is a genial subject for a sermon, it proceeds with order and is a great help both in disposing the audience, and in giving the speaker a certain animation, as it makes him foresee the fruit of the seed.

I, on the contrary, come to you, as St. Paul said of himself, *in weakness, in fear, and in trembling;* not on your account in particular (for we have better and more salutary hopes for you) but on account of the experience we have of retreats in general and of the little change they work.

Will you make an exception, Ladies? That, God only knows, He who gives growth to the work of those who plant and water.

Our experience is always sad, and it leads us to-day to speak . . . Of the inutility of the retreat.

Without doubt it is written: that it is there that God speaks to the heart, and the word of God lives eternally. But it is also written: that God waits at the door, that He knocks, and if *any one hears His voice and opens the door.* . . . Hence He leaves it to our liberty to listen or not to hear; to open or to shut the door of our heart!

The inutility of the retreat does not come from God and His grace . . . no one is deprived of this grace; God stands always at the door, knocks, and wants to enter.

I do not wish to tell you that the inutility of the retreat comes from me, my weakness, my incapacity, my unworthiness. All this is only too true, and if I were fully convinced of it, this truly humble feeling would be a guarantee of success. To display this feeling would be mock humility, which is neither solid nor of good dye. Besides, let the aqueduct be of lead, wood or stone, its pipes encrusted with sediment, that does not prevent the water, which it distributes, from reaching the reservoir pure.

Let us say it frankly, and for the greater profit to your souls: the inutility of the retreat comes from you; the audience in general is unapproachable, unteachable, exacting and aggressive.

1st. What in reality is a gathering of ladies for a retreat? If I mistake not, it is the gathering of the most regular, most pious and fervent women.

And it is for this reason that the retreat is often *completely useless*.

For there are only two things to be preached: the truths that lead to conversion and those you do not need; or the truths that lead to improvement and progress. Pious persons think they do not need to be improved: in general they have great confidence in themselves, their justice, and their regularity.

It is the error of piety, and this error, my God! it is very difficult to prevent.

First of all, there is such moral weakness in this age, that for whatever little one does, one is exalted as perfect.

Take for example a man, especially in a high social position, who goes to mass, oh! very regular, . . . but . . .

Or a woman who is a weekly communicant, she is a saint . . . but . . .

For instance how can you expect a woman, who does not dance during Lent, not to think herself perfect by the side of so many women who think they have done admirably well in not dancing during Passion week, or that a woman who only half spoils her children should reproach herself, when so many adore them like idols and tremble before them; that a woman who is only half immodest should not think herself very exemplary, when so many others, pious in a way, keep within no bounds?

Difficult audience, which is neither to be converted nor improved, which thinks itself perfect, and has some reason to think so!

This is the first cause of the inutility of retreats.

"You are like," says Jesus Christ, "those children[1] sitting in the market place, crying to their companions," saying: " we have piped to you and you

[1] Matt., xi, 16, 17.

have not danced; we have lamented and you have not mourned!"

Ah! among you, ladies, the seed of the divine word falls neither by the way-side, nor on rocky ground, but it falls among thorns which choke its growth.

2nd. To this particular disposition of the audience is added a general one, which makes us despair for the result . . . and you do not escape this: it is in the air of independence which we breathe in these days.

The christian pulpit is no longer a seat of teaching, with authority; it is a tribune where the talent of speech exercises itself more or less, and produces more or less pleasure, surprise or emotion on the hearer. The word of God is received as though it were the word of man.

Neither have we *disciples* any longer before the pulpit, that is to say, those whom one teaches and who come to be taught.

Absolute disciples, like children at school or at college; in fact, have we any there now? . . .

There is not even that *semi-docility* which one finds at the foot of the pulpit, of the sciences, and the arts, where the hearer recognizes at least a certain superiority of light and of official authority to teach. . . . We no longer have disciples, there, where docility should be complete.

What have we then? *Critics?* Let us not speak of it, let us cast aside this worn-out reproach. Let la Bruyère tell us that the fruit of a sermon is to judge between the first and the second point, between the one of to-day and the one which preceded it. . . . The critic, presupposes concentrated attention, the deepest interest, it is not our radical evil.

We have *only amateurs.* They come, they pose, they go away *en amateur;* they come to seek talent, pleasure and emotion, just as they would go to a concert; they go away bored or enchanted; but the word of God is no more a mistress to teach, to produce remorse, fruit, reform or improvement, than the play of the actor, the action of the public improvisatore, or the voice and talent of the artist.

And you are going to cry out, to say: "it will not be so with us." Ladies, this is the basis of the audience . . . *amateurs.* . . . We no longer have disciples who come to be taught and directed.

3rd. New cause of the inutility of the retreat; the amateur audience is very exacting. First of all it does not want *dogma*.

Besides, it knows it,—God grant it!—It is annoying to be sure, for when it is a question of the Creed, or of the doctrinal part of the Sacraments, there is nothing to deduct, not a word to retrench.

We do not want this double pendulum in equilibrium, where in meditating on what God has done for us, we conclude what we should do for Him, where we animate and vivify our fidelity in proportion to the commands and benefits of the Lord.

We prefer, for instance, to crawl in a sort of mutilated half measure, in abstinences without depth or motive, rather than to persuade ourselves of the authority of the Church, its vivifying motives, its prolific reasons, and by this means to be conducted into the spirit, the entire letter and exact fervour of penance.

Secondly, the audience only wants ethics.

Because ethics in its rules, deductions and applications presents different points of view, there you think there is bargaining with God, compromises to be made, agreements, accommodations with heaven;

and you even want the ethics a *little vague,* something from which you can take or leave.

You want to hear *penance* preached, provided each one is allowed to do as little of it as possible;—*modesty in dress,* provided that the application of it, is left to the artist who makes the costumes;—*respect for Sunday,* provided that each one may dispose of the day to her fancy;—*alms,* provided that one limits oneself to certain social duties;—*employment of time,* provided that an indolent useless life is not blamed;—*education of the children,* provided that they may be just as much idolized after the sermon, after the retreat, as before.

But if we attempt to specify the rules of abstinence and fast, and to lead from that to the spirit of penance and renunciation, it is a doctrine which is no longer accepted.

If we attack the style of dress when you dress like others, even though others may dress in such a way as to make even the world laugh, that sermon is hard, and no one can listen to it.

If in the observation of Sunday, we specify to the extent of taking from your fingers, so idle during the week, a needle or a crochet, you cry out against an exaggerated severity.

If we indicate a perfect means of regulating alms with order, and with security for your conscience, immediately we encroach on the liberty of the application.

If we demonstrate to you that life should be useful in all things, and that you have not the liberty of doing nothing nor of occupying your time with nothings, you cry out at the intolerance which wishes to lead you to a cloistered life.

Finally, if we point out to you your unpardonable weakness in the education, and fatal adoration of those little idols whom you dress up to-day, and before whom you will tremble to-morrow, it is encroaching on forbidden ground.

Hence with such a vague preaching, with ethics without support, without any precise application that is practical or useful, we ruin all the utility of the word of God, and the best of retreats become useless.

4th. The audience itself attacks the word of God and thus achieves the inutility of a retreat by its aggressive tendency.

The attack is not straightforward, not with the club of the unbeliever or the impious man, the sardonic laugh of the libertine, or of the light and indifferent man (that sort of an attack could easily be repelled), but it is made with hidden, incisive arms, such as it takes the delicacy of woman to handle. They have wounded, says the prophet,[1] "as a sharp razor."

It is Delilah cutting the hair of Samson and taking all his strength.

To explain myself:

The ethics which we preach is addressed to all, and in speaking to all, it produces in its exactness a perfectly good rule, because it is true and just.

But this rule is modified according to circumstances, position and difficulties.

For example, a dance is improper and dangerous; we are obliged to declare it such from the pulpit.— But, such a one cannot give it up without causing great tumult in the household; besides she makes the exercise as slightly improper as possible, and considering her character and temperament, the danger becomes very remote; then the rule published in all its truth modifies itself with real wisdom.

This moral law, then, which should be given as a general and sure rule, will often undergo a curve

[1] Psalm LI, 4.

of inflection in passing through the centre of particular positions and each one who is exempt only thinking of herself, finds the true principle exaggerated, owing to the modifications which a prudent direction has brought to it. She questions it from the pulpit to the confessional, from the preacher to the director, she confuses all, ruins all.

Instead of saying she is the exception, she says she is the rule, she does not admit of refractions, of different centres in the road of light, and exclaiming for all in a shrill, sharp voice, she easily ruins the fruit of a lesson which has kept in the most exact limits.

Ladies, there is only one tribune for the word of God, let it be called pulpit or confessional; the first gives the law to all, the second applies to the individual the exception which proves the rule, but nowhere are there two weights and two measures. The stick which I plunge in the water, and which seems to curve, does not really do so, it is an optical effect, that is all; it is your position seen from a different point of view than the general one.

You would not believe how much this *confusion* attacks and ruins the word of God.

The spirit of independence which has penetrated everywhere is a new attack.

Formerly, when the heart of man left truths in their entirety, he said:

"I do not *wish*," if the conscience revolted against God, but a moment might come when he might say, " My heart is ready, Lord, my heart is ready, speak, because your servant listens."

He said: "I *can* not." It was the cry of laziness, but he might have come to this word: "I can do all, in Him who fortifies me. Cannot I do what this or that one does?"

He said: "I *dare* not." It was the voice of weakness and human respect, but he might have become brave, have armed his heart and proved himself strong.

He said: "*Later*, later, to-morrow, to-morrow," and this to-morrow might have changed into *to-day*.

But in our days, the spirit of independence has *diminished* the truths, has undermined and mutilated them to its own level; to be in the rule we make the rule bend to us, and we say: "*I need not*, I am not obliged, there is no obligation, I am in line, in order, there is nothing to correct, to change, to improve in me."

What can we do, what can we hope for with such a sharp, decided independence?

Instead of acknowledging that you are not in the rule, of mourning over it, of reproaching yourselves for the abuse of the grace of God; you make a rule for yourselves, running over the globe to find a doctor whom you entice by dint of illusion, or by creating difficulties and exemptions. "All you do is right, all you desire is holy." Ruinous disposition which renders the word of God useless; it runs in vain, it strikes the air without success, and you ask the prophets to tell you that which pleases you. In short, this theology which you make for yourselves (for who is not a theologian nowadays) meets in *real* theology a false support, which succeeds in ruining all; I should take this prop, which leads to what is false only, from you, Ladies.

Theology, which is the rule of religious science, has been confounded, probably on purpose, with the *exhortation of the ministry*, which directs the customs, habits, and works of religious conduct.

Theology proceeds by decisions, it declares what is permitted or forbidden, of duty or counsel, of precise obligation or religious decorum; besides, on each point it weighs the grave or light nature of the sin. And I am pleased every time that, with the light of God and the inspiration of the Church, I see it take off this weight grain by grain, which in the divine balance would incline the scale into the abyss.

But, by the side of this sovereignly respectable theology, which is just and merciful like the Lord, there is the exhortation of the ministry, which desires with prudence, that souls should not remain in this perilous balance on the trembling limit of divine anger, which urges them to do a little more than bare duty for this God, whom they should love with all their hearts, and which tries to form in hearts customs of religion, habits of piety, over and above the rules which constitute mortal sins.

Only to mention some points,—it is this *exhortation* which has formed the habit of night and morning prayers, of the *Angelus*, of Grace before and after meals, of the parochial Mass, the sermon, the Office of Vespers, the sanctification of the solemn days of Holy Week, of frequent Communion; although on these points and others, there is no strict obligation, but a simple counsel.

Though if only what is of strict obligation is desired, if we are always to be calculating on what *we do not owe to God,* you understand that all exhortation, all direction, should cease, because it becomes useless.

If religious precept is always to be thrown at us to condemn exhortation which counsels and engages; it is to confuse all religious ideas, to paralyze all religious feeling.

If you translate purposely what is only exhortation into imposed obligation, in order to *inure* the stigma of severity, sometimes the disgrace of error, you ruin all the good the word of God can produce. And after having made a theology for yourselves, in order to do the least possible, you make use of theological precision to justify yourselves in doing scarcely anything.

Was I not right, Ladies, in insisting upon the inutility of the retreat?

What shall be the practical conclusion now? For you to go back to your usual habits, and me also; to finish the retreat before having scarcely begun it? No.

1st. To persuade yourselves that you have the greatest need of improvement, change, and conversion even, in a certain sense;

2nd. To constitute yourselves docile disciples and not amateur judges or critics;

3d. To esteem dogma, to desire ethics, in its most incisive deductions, for your reform; to love the light that shines, and the truth that teaches;

4th. Not to confound the exception with the rule, not to make a theology of your own, nor to call it to the rigour of duty, to ruin christian customs.

At this rate the retreat will be useful.

I exhort you, then, not to receive the grace of God in vain; for a happy cultivated land that drinks often of the dew of heaven, and in spite of all its advantages produces thorns and thistles is reproved, says St. Paul, it is very near to malediction. Let me add quickly with the apostle, that I have better hopes for you, hopes bordering on salvation, although I speak in such a way, in order to lead you to God.

THE ABUSE OF GRACES.

Succide ficulneam, utquid etiam terram occupat?
"Cut it down therefore, why cumbereth it the ground" Luke, XIII, 7.

LADIES, when they wish to build on rocky ground, they commence by using the pick, and often by blasting the stony difficulties which prevent the placing of the foundation of the edifice.

That is what we did in speaking of the *inutility* of the retreat, and of the hard obstacles which hinder the edification of the work of grace. If you find that I have employed a frightening explosive, if, even at a distance, you have been struck by some of the splinters, they are the wounds of one who loves, the darts of charity which strike and cure.

But in order to clear the ground entirely, to reach the bottom, so as to build seriously and solidly, it is still necessary to dig, break, and remove much ruggedness: we must meditate on a subject which is nothing more than the conclusion of the preceding one, viz. : *the abuse of graces.*

Certainly, the errors which I have pointed out to you constitute the greatest abuse of the grace of God; it is abuse at its source; but there still remains the abuse of habitual graces.

Here the tree is not uprooted as it is by the inutility of the word of God and the retreat,—but it neither profits by the air, the sun, nor the dew, and occupying uselessly the ground, Jesus Christ threatens to cut it down, *succede ficulneam.*

I.

THE CRIME OF THE ABUSE OF GRACES.

There is one rule which cannot mislead, that is the Gospel. The portraits which Jesus Christ has engraved and stereotyped there, will be the same until the consummation of time. All the miseries which the Saviour has filed out before Him, the merciful or severe judgment which He has pronounced on them, are the ineffable types of our miseries and of the judgment which Jesus Christ will pronounce on us.

There is one remarkable thing about the Holy Gospel, that is, that it is the breath of gentleness, indulgence and pardon. All sinners are received kindly: the woman taken in adultery, the light and unbelieving Samaritan woman, the prodigal son, the son who refused to obey but immediately repaired his disobedience, Zachary soiled with the goods of others, the thief with his hands stained with blood . . . . all . . . . to the extent that they murmured: "This man receives sinners and eats with them; he is the friend of sinners and publicans."

To the extent that piety, misunderstood, and even the world, which does not pique itself on being over scrupulous, is surprised, not to say scandalized.

But beyond this indulgence, carried to the last limit, we distinguish three miseries which have incurred an almost unpardonable severity. We hear only three times the word woe, malediction, *Vae vobis!*

Woe to the world and to the rich, *Vae mundo et divitibus!*

Woe to pharisaical hypocrisy, *Vae vobis, Pharisaeis!*

Woe to the abuse of graces, *Vae tibi, Corozain!*

This is not the place, Ladies, to tell you in what a true sense (and a consoling one for you who escape the anathema), Jesus Christ said: "Woe to the scandals of the world and the abuse of riches!" to justify the anathema pronounced against hypocrisy, which trifles with God and man. . . .

We shall have quite enough to do to-day, to examine the seal of divine reprobation on the abuse of graces. Listen:

"Then began He to upbraid the cities wherein were done the most of His miracles, for that they had not done penance!"[1]

"Woe to thee, Corozain! Woe to thee, Bethsaida! for if in Tyre and Sidon had been wrought the miracles that have been wrought in you, they had long ago done penance in sackcloth and ashes. But I say unto you, it shall be more tolerable for Tyre and Sidon in the day of judgment than for you."

"And thou, Capharnaum . . . . for if in Sodom had been wrought the miracles that have been wrought in thee, perhaps it had remained unto this day. But I say unto you, that it shall be more

[1] Matt., II, 20, 21, 22, 23, 24.

tolerable for the land of Sodom in the day of judgment than for thee."

"The men of Nineveh shall rise in judgment with this generation and shall condemn it; because they did penance at the preaching of Jonas, and behold a greater than Jonas here."[1]

"The queen of the South shall rise up in judgment with this generation and shall condemn it; because she came from the ends of the earth to hear the wisdom of Solomon, and behold a greater than Solomon here."

"*Amen I say* to you."[2]

"The publicans and harlots shall go into the kingdom of God before you."

"Therefore I say to you, that the kingdom of God shall be taken from you, and shall be given to a nation yielding the fruits thereof."

This same God said by his prophet: "My beloved had a vineyard on a hill in a fruitful place. And he fenced it in, and picked the stones out of it, and planted it with the choicest vines, and built a tower in the midst thereof, and set up a wine press therein: and he looked that it should bring forth grapes, and

[1] Matt., xii, 41, 42. [2] Matt., xi, 31, 43.

it brought forth wild grapes. And now, O ye inhabitants of Jerusalem, and ye men of Juda, judge between me and my vineyard. What is there that I ought to do more to my vineyard, that I have not done to it? Was it that I looked that it should bring forth grapes and it hath brought forth wild grapes? And now I will show you what I will do to my vineyard. I will take away the hedge thereof, and it shall be wasted; and I will break down the wall thereof, and it shall be trodden down, and I will make it desolate; it shall not be pruned, and it shall not be digged, but briars and thorns shall come up, and I will command the clouds to rain no rain upon it."[1]

Perhaps you think you are not this cursed vine; at least you will recognize yourselves in the following picture:

"Ten acres of vineyard," said the Lord, "shall yield one little measure, and thirty bushels of seed shall yield three measure."[2]

Add to these terrible threats the parable of the hired vine, the planters of which were lost; the parable of the hidden talent, which is taken from

[1] Isaiah, v, 1, 2, 3, 4, 5, 6.   [2] Isaiah, v, 10.

the negligent possessor; the parable of the wedding feast of a king's son, from which the guests excused themselves on account of their business and their pleasure, and are thrown into exterior darkness.

And you will understand that the abuse of grace is a crime, since it has the curse of God and the most terrible result for eternity.

II.

IN WHAT THE ABUSE OF GRACES CONSISTS.

1st. It does not consist in that human *weakness* which is always offending God, in spite of good intentions, and above all, in spite of the sorrow which one feels,—but in that determined resolution not to do, not to go further, to do the least possible, not to think oneself obliged, and in this disposition to allow these torrents of grace which inundate us, to run around, near, and in us, as a slanting roof allows the rain to strike it, without retaining it. It is to make oneself callous, to cauterize the conscience, and no longer feel the price of grace.

2nd. It does not consist only in the abuse of the graces of salvation, *properly speaking*,—for example, in the abuse of the word of God, which falls everywhere like rain, in the superior and voluntary resistance of these words, in the withdrawing from a retreat which presents itself, from the sacraments, which we have every facility to receive; in the disregard of examples which accompany us in our family, as the shadow follows the body, of events which warn us, of age which speaks very loud to us, of holy desires, of good impulses, of generous inspirations which God puts in our hearts.

This abuse is caused, principally, by the abuse of *common* graces, for which one has no remorse, to which people in the world do not even pay attention.

They abuse the resources of their fortune by spending it all on themselves and their pleasures, without any remorse. A man whose narrow and egotistical life is spent in taking care of, and in increasing his *own* goods, is looked upon as a man whose existence is amply justified.

They abuse the gifts of the intellect to become sluggards, useless beings, epicures, at best frivolous readers, and they think, without remorse, that God gave them all the gifts of the mind for this only.

They abuse the wealth of education in taking from it the independence of all authority, the horror of any yoke; and when God has showered all earthly gifts on them, it is then that they think themselves justified in doing nothing, and in suffering nothing for Him.

And after having abused all; lessons, advice, examples, fortune, intellect, education, goods of every nature, only to think of self, only to see self, only to seek self, can one expect to find oneself well disposed to profit by the word of salvation? Error. Begin by being a woman who does not abuse the gifts of nature and the world, and you will reach the point of not abusing the gifts of grace.

3d. And are not we timid preachers of the Gospel, the ones who encourage this abuse of graces by handling them differently from the Apostles and the Fathers?

We are about to discuss some inches of dress;

Some steps of the dance;

Some stitches for Sunday;

Some sensualities of lenten evenings;

Some respect for the seriousness of lent; and we proceed like those who take off a painful sticking-plaster by degrees, and make the sick cry out, instead of taking it off with one pull.

Awkward ones! We are going to ask all this of *christian women*, who give no heed to an indolent, idle, sensual, egotistical life, who have hearts which are neither void of the love of the world,

Nor filled with the love of God.

Let us say plainly, with St. John: "Do not love the world, nor the things of the world."

Let us say plainly, with the Saviour: "Thou shalt love the Lord thy God with all thy heart."

Then, all pulling *ceasing*, you will be less exposed to abuse the graces of God.

"A certain man," said the Saviour in parable, "had a fig-tree planted in his vineyard, and he came seeking fruit on it and found none."[1]

"And he said to the dresser of the vineyard: Behold, for three years I come seeking fruit on this fig-tree and I find none. Cut it down therefore; why cumbereth it the ground."

"But he answering, said to him: Lord, let it alone *this year* also, until I dig about it and dung

[1] Luke, XIII, 6, 7, 8, 9.

it, and if happily, it bear fruit; but if not, then after that thou shalt cut it down."

Ladies, the application is simple, but terrible; if, hearing to-day, this year, the voice of the Lord you harden your hearts; if God could say this sad word in presenting Himself to the children whom he has already loaded with graces: "Behold, these have altogether broken the yoke more: *Et hi magis fregerunt jugum.*" [1]

---

[1] Jeremiah, v, 5.

THE LOVE OF GOD.

> *Fundamentum aliud nemo potest ponere*
> *praeter id quod positum est*
> "For other foundation no man can lay,
> but that which is laid " I Cor , III, 11.

AFTER having made deep excavations, by giving the word of God and the retreat their active use,—after all, the clearing away which a more holy use of grace operates—our work is to lay the foundation of the edifice of salvation.

There is no other than the one laid by God Himself in the law, which the Holy Ghost has written in our hearts, which Jesus Christ has proclaimed as essential to possess eternal life; the love of God above every thing; consequently, hatred of the world, and all in the world that might weaken or extinguish the love of God.

We resist, refuse, fight and dispute the ground inch by inch; there are a thousand pullings and haulings on this foundation, and what we give, we give reluctantly, unwillingly, and in the smallest degree.

The love of God is the only stone large and strong enough to occupy all the ground cleared in our hearts, to carry on its solid surface all the weight of the edifice of salvation.

But shall we first drive out the love of the world to establish the love of God, or shall we place the love of God at once, so that the love of the world will find the place filled?

The second is preferable.

For the heart must always be full; one affection will drive out the other. If you empty it before filling it, it will think itself dead in its moments of moral asphyxia; when the heart, without loving the world, will not love God. The empty vanity of the world should be chased out by the love of God, which alone is capable of filling the heart, as the vacuum of air, which occupied the capacity of a vase, is naturally chased out the instant you fill the vase with water or a vivifying liquid.

Besides, the work would be interminable if we began by chasing out the love of the world. The heart not yet loving God, and loving the world a great deal, would only detach itself with cries from its foolish and close affections one by one. It would be an adherent appliance which could only be removed by tearing the cuticle, the sacrifice of a cargo at sea, when there is no indication of a storm, furniture of which we are very fond thrown from the window when the height of the fire does not make it necessary. "Set fire to the house," says St. Francis de Sales, "and it will empty itself very quickly; set the heart on fire with the love of God, and the love of the world will fly before its flames, which would soon have consumed it, had it not seen fit to empty the places."

I.

We do not question the fact that we must love God, but we prefer not to occupy ourselves with it, so that, admitting it as a vague principle, it will not interfere with anything in practice.

All will grant you this obligation, just as they grant that there are seven stars in the Great Bear Constellation; one of these truths having no more influence than the other on the direction of our conduct.

But that the love of God is the foundation, and the only foundation, of salvation; that it is the first and greatest of all the commandments; that to observe it is life, and not to observe it is death; that it resumes in itself all the law, all the exhortations of the prophets, all the word of God; finally, that the answer to the greatest, the most essential, the most vital question: "Master, what must I do to possess life eternal?" is this, "Thou shalt love the Lord thy God with all thy heart." This is what is not understood, and when it is understood is not meditated on; and when meditated on, is practised in the most pitiable manner.

II.

What, then, is the love of God? This is what we must now thoroughly penetrate ourselves with.

1st. It is not that sensible and *affectionate* attraction which the heart feels for creatures whom we see, hear, and communicate with. The love of God is not of the same nature, for example, as the sensible love of a mother for her little child. And St. John makes us understand this distinction, when he says: "For he that loveth not his brother whom *he seeth*, how can he love God whom *he seeth not?*"[1]

This confusion of a sensible love, given to a spiritual and invisible being, is what frightens and discourages so many souls; is what makes them think that the love of God is impossible, because they understand it in the gross and material sense of those movements of the heart towards visible and created objects.

The delicious sentiment of an effective love which electrifies Pauls, Francis Xaviers, Teresas, Madelaines of Pazzi, is not given to all, it is refused to the greater number; it is rather the anticipated recompense of divine love, than the essential life of this love diffused into our hearts by the Holy Ghost.

2nd. The love of God, is the habitual *preference* given to God over all creatures;—frank determination to prefer God to all things, to sacrifice all that would turn us from His grace by sin.

Remark that I do not say *preference actually given, sacrifice actually* made of everything; that would be *impeccability*; this love is reserved for

[1] I John, IV, 20.

heaven,—but *habitual* disposition, determination—for there are persons who avoid certain faults who fulfil certain duties; but for all that they have not this *habitual preference*. While *on* the other *hand*, there are those who have this determination, and still fall into certain faults without losing the essence of the love of God, which consists in the readiness of the heart to sacrifice everything.

One example will explain all, on a point of such importance and which is so little understood.

Blanche of Castile must have loved St. Louis, as you love your children, with that same tenderness of heart, that same fire of affection which consumes you; there is *affectionate* love of a mother according to nature. But when Blanche said to her son: "My son, God knows how I love you, nevertheless I would rather see you deprived of life and of the beautiful Kingdom of France than guilty of one mortal sin." There is the love of preference for God in the heart of the mother according to grace. Remark, however, that Blanche did not say "*I prefer*," that would be presumption in such a delicate choice; she says "*I would prefer*," I am, by grace in that disposition, and if her heart wavered sometimes in this heroic comparison of the two loves (comparison which it is not always prudent to make), Blanche, even in the midst of maternal weaknesses, had the true essence of the love of God in her heart.

This virtual and habitual *preference* is a very grave point of examen, Ladies; and as long as the heart does not attain it, the love of God is not in the heart.

3d. This positive preference is not something *vague*,—left to the capriciousness of sentiment—it consists in an indicated sacrifice, determined by the things forbidden us by the commandments, and by the duties which they impose. "If any one loves Me, he will keep My word." "If you love Me, keep My commandments." "He who keeps the precepts is he who loves Me." Love is as strong as death; and as death separates the body from created objects, so love separates the heart from disorderly affection for creatures. The love of God is that we keep His commandments. He who says: "I love, and does not keep My precepts, is a liar." The proof of love, is shown by our works. We really love God if we cut ourselves off from our guilty pleasures to envelope ourselves in His law. The worship of God, is the love of Him.

And this is the very nature of love, for if any one pretended to love us, and acted towards us as we act towards God, showing no preference either for us, our desires, or our wishes, we should never believe in his love.

This preference, then, is something very positive; when I force myself, for the love of God, to keep His commandments, I prefer God and the love I owe Him, to the disorderly love for creatures, which draws me and wishes to lead me; I prefer God to self-interest and violence, which would make me profane His holy name; to gain and independence, which would make me profane His holy day; to pride, which would prevent me from submitting to those He has placed over me; I prefer it to anger and vengeance, to the allurement of guilty pleasures, to the cupidity that violates the rights of others, to the gain of lying, to bad desires and avarice, which would check almsgiving; I prefer it to my indifference, which would keep me far from the sources of grace; I prefer it to my liberty and my sensuality, which would wish to use time and supplies, without any reserve or payment for the sovereign Master.

4th. This preference of the heart constitues the first commandment.

For what does: You shall love me with all your heart, with all your soul, with all your mind, and with all your strength, mean? I love you with all my heart, means unquestionably: I give you the preference above everybody and everything.

It is love, not sovereign by intensity or sensation, but by appreciation, and it is the only possible, true, and exacted love.

Susanna loved God with all her heart when she said: "I am straightened on every side; for if I do this thing it is death to me, and if I do it not, I shall not escape your hands. But it is better for me to fall into your hands without doing it, than to sin in the sight of the Lord."[1]

The Theban legion loved God with all its heart, when it said to Maximian, by the mouth of St. Maurice: "We are your soldiers, and we owe you military service; but we are the servants of God, and we owe Him the innocence of our souls. You

[1] Daniel, XIII, 23.

wish to make us renounce this innocence; we prefer to renounce life."

Blanche of Castile, as we have seen, was a mother who loved God with all her heart, when she preferred to sacrifice to grace, her maternal love, the life of her son and his brilliant heritage in the world.

These, love God with all their heart: the merchant who closes his shop on Sunday at the risk of competition and loss; the christian workman who exposes himself to the threats of no longer being occupied rather than violate the holy day; the young man who affronts human respect rather than break his abstinence; the warrior who tramples the world under foot rather than attack the life of his brother in a hand-to-hand combat; the woman who triumphs over all, even her heart, rather than live an instant in a delicate situation.

And you, you love God with all your heart each time that you give this sovereign quality to contrition, which is essential to it, and say to God from the depth of your heart: "Death rather than offend Thee."

5th. This preference of the heart and of the will is not only the nature, it is the substance of the first commandment. It is only filled when the heart is disposed to prefer God to all else.

Notwithstanding this, of all things, the first commandment is the most neglected; it seems only to figure in the decalogue *for form*, and when we examine ourselves on this great legislation: "One God only shalt thou adore, shalt thou love *perfectly;*" the examination ends in asking ourselves, if we have missed our morning or evening prayers.

Those who are most attentive pass in review their religious exercises; for the heart, there is never a question. The love of God, says Fenelon, seems an onerous debt, but vaguely established: we try to elude it by formalities and an exterior worship, which we always endeavour to put in the place of that sincere and effective love,—we feel that there is a void to fill, that we honour God only in loving Him; and to fill the void, we heap up practices and the gain of indulgences.

About as you do, Ladies, when some one is announced who annoys and tires you: after the first sensation of ill-humour or displeasure, you compose yourselves very quickly through politeness (and a little through vanity), and cover with gracious formalities, which are sometimes exaggerated, the void which the inopportune visit still gnaws in your heart. I do not blame this worldly charity, it is polite and kind; only I compare it with all those formalities and practices heaped up to fill the void in your hearts with regard to God.

Yes, the most barren thing in the christian life, is this fidelity to the first and the greatest commandment.

In beginning at the bottom of the religious ladder, the first category comprises those who pretend to be faithful to the 5th and 7th commandments;

The second category, admits the 5th, 7th and 8th;

The third, the 5th, 7th, 8th and 6th.

The fourth, the 5th, 7th, 8th, 6th, 4th, 3d, and 2nd commandments.

As to the 9th and 10th, they are scarcely thought of, because they refer to interior acts.

As to the commandments of the church, we place the *echo* of the voice of God far below the *voice* itself.

But for the first commandment no one troubles oneself; it is filled by duties of *adoration* more or less restrained; more or less multiplied.

Do you hear those distressing groans as soon as it is question of doing something for God; and that joy which celebrates a triumph and a good fortune, when the Church has just lessened a penitential rule?

Do you hear all that agitation of pious souls, all those discussions, researches, interrogations, in order to see how to do the least possible? I have never seen the consultors hesitate over doing *too much*, and all the phrases of consultation are formed thus: "*Isn't it so, that we are not obliged?*"

Do you hear that shameful expression that habit has sanctioned? *Done as if for the love of God!* Open the official code of the French language, and you will read: "Said in speaking of a thing done or given unwillingly, with sordidness; example: You look as though you were working for the love of God." Ah! Ladies, this expression should not be French since it is neither generous nor christian; it should be our work to abolish it.

Ah! truly, if you had a servant who served you as you serve God, doing the least possible, always discussing obligations, and doing the indispensable "*comme pour l'amour de Dieu;*" if, in addition, this servant maintained that she loved you with all her heart, you would think that she was insulting you; at any rate, you would not keep her in your service *a week*.

Alas! if God the Creator did only the indispensable for us, what should we have? Bread and water for nourishment, some yards of stuff for clothing, some twisted branches for habitation! If God the Redeemer did only the indispensable for us, what should we have? Baptism; then guard yourselves to carry this garment without spot to His tribunal! If God the Sanctifier did only the indispensable for us, what should we have? Some strictly necessary graces, a movement once imprinted, then: go as you have been started!

Oh! instead of decapitating the decalogue and making a lifeless corpse of it, leave it its *head*, that head which is the seat and source of life; and see, with this vital love, the quickening and fruitful principles circulating in all the precepts:

Faithful honour and reparation for the holy name of God;

The Lord's day kept and delicately observed;

The family in order and happy;

The duties of state of life religiously followed;

Charity superabounding and victorious over evil;

Purity of heart united with purity of customs;

Noble probity carried to the extent of disinterestedness and alms;

Egoism killed and left lifeless;

Respect for the reputation of our neighbour;

Mediocrity esteemed more than gold;

And moderation in his desires, crowning the happiness of man.

There is the love of God, Ladies, such as it should reign in your hearts, if you wish to fill the first commandment.

Do not let us deceive ourselves about it.

There is no religion without the love of God, *non colitur Deus nisi amando.*

We must love God in everything and above everything if we wish to have sincere piety.

And what does all this mean? the *preference of the heart, and this preference given to God.*

We must reach this point not only through *fear,* but through effective and appreciative *love.*

We can even go from this to a certain joy, a certain happiness, at least a certain peace, in the midst of sacrifices made for the God loved and preferred;—for, where one loves, is no fatigue, or if there is labour, the work is loved.

It costs so little when we love the creature!

Shall it cost much then to love that which we have loved too late and too little?

THE FLIGHT OF THE LOVE OF THE WORLD.

> *Ortus est sol . . . . exhibit homo ad opus suum.*
> "The sun ariseth . . man shall go forth to his work and to his labour till evening." Psalm CIII, 22–23.

LADIES, have you sometimes seen on autumn mornings a beautiful view encroached upon and saddened by a dense fog? The eye cannot distinguish anything in this uniform atmosphere, which shrouds the green prairie, the winding serpentine river, the rising hill, and the valley rich with habitations. The fresh wind cannot chase this fog away,—it can only disperse it, and another foggy layer will immediately occupy the vacated space. But some hours after, the sun pierces through, and from on high, holds dominion over all this damp dust, and divides and absorbs it, when the view again takes all the animation of its natural physiognomy.

This fog is the love of the world, which disfigures everything, and leaves unhealthy miasmas behind it. The wind is the word of God, which can only push and displace. The sun is the love of God, which disperses and reëstablishes everything.

We can say of the love of the world what David said of night: "Thou hast appointed darkness, and it is night; in it shall all the beasts of the world go about."[1] Let us add that we see thieves, evil-doers and vagabonds going about also .... We can also say of the love of God what the prophet adds: "The sun riseth and they are gathered together and they shall lie down in their dens. Man shall go forth to his work and to his labour till evening." The return of the light does more to disperse the evil-doers than all the patrol of armed force during the night. So is the love of God the great means of putting to flight the love of the world.

Put this *preference* (of which we spoke) in a heart, and it will no longer be necessary to preach against

[1] Psalm CIII, 20, 22, 23.

the contrary affection,—to discuss the principle, to dispute the possession of the heart. This is the reason why it was first necessary to place the love of God, in order to destroy the love of the world.

This destruction is the forced consequence of divine love, and at the same time the fertile means of keeping up its activity.

I.

YOU SHOULD NOT LOVE THE WORLD.

It is the greatest enemy to the preference which we owe to God.

Here are the two adversaries which rend the heart; this heart which, like the butterfly, flutters around the trembling light in a small room where night has been made, at the risk of burning and destroying itself; if you open the window wide, if you let the air and sun penetrate the room, it will fly away, happy in the clear azure and will rest only on the perfume of flowers.

You should not love the world.

Do not let us discuss the continual excursions which you make in the world.

I accord a great deal, in according that you do no wrong there, that you cause none by your dress and your dancing.

I grant that you are much protected : 1st, by temperament, ordinarily more calm in you than the heart and the imagination ; 2nd, by reserve, which is more familiar to you, and more imposed ; 3d, by habit, which blunts a great deal ; 4th, above all, by a powerful inheritance, coquetry, that vanity which makes you more occupied with dress than with beauty, with yourself and praises, than with evil.

I, above all, grant that you do no wrong, in the gross sense in which the world understands it, which is unwilling to take into consideration the disorders of the heart, of the imagination, and perhaps of something much less spiritualized.

Neither is the question at this moment, to know if you should go in the world or not, in what manner, and to what extent you should participate in its customs and its allurements.

The question is of an incontestable principle ; it is that you should not *love the world*, even in going in it, even in posing there, either as a simple spectator or as a fashionable and much-sought-after actor.

The word of the beloved disciple answers all, ends all discussions: "Little children, love not the world, nor the things which are in the world."[1]

You should not love the world because Jesus Christ condemned it: "Woe to the world on account of its scandals." "I pray not for the world, Father! I pray not that thou shouldst take them out of the world, but that thou shouldst keep them from evil."[2]

Because you renounced the world in your baptism, you said anathema to it; for what are the pomps of the devil, if not ambition, arrogance, superfluity in the use of human things?

Because the love of the world is not reconcilable with the love of God. "Whosoever, therefore, will be a friend of this world, becometh an enemy of God."[3] And, on the other hand, he who claims to be the friend of God, by that declares himself the enemy of the world.

II.

YOU CANNOT LOVE THE WORLD.

For this it is sufficient to know what is meant by the world, and how unworthy it is of our love.

[1] I John, II, 15.   [2] John, XVII, 3.   [3] James, IV, 4.

It is not human society, which God founded and blessed. Neither is it your reunions, taken in themselves and stripped of all that makes them anti-christian; they have nothing to condemn them in themselves, they may even strengthen ties and produce necessary relaxation.

The world of which the Gospel speaks, is in the midst of the material and social world, a seductive, persecuting, corrupting world, which believes, thinks, speaks, professes, and acts against God, against His truth and His law; a world all plunged in vice; a world where all is concupiscence of the flesh and of the eye, pride of life. A world, in consequence, which stirs everywhere, in the parlour as in the smoky tavern, in the literary circle as in the work-shop, in the country as in the town.

That is the world which I say you *cannot* love, not on account of all that results from it, which is bitter for you, intrigues, humiliations, competitions, disgust, ingratitude, deceptions, tears, pitiless harshness (you could preach a thousand times better on that than I), but on account of the evil in which it is plunged, and in which it plunges you.

For remark, that by the world we do not mean the *sinner drawn* by human weakness, or by the corruption of nature, but the *worldling*, systematically *opposed* to the Gospel.

Do you think, christian women, that you *can* love that world? See it always in opposition to Jesus Christ; only to speak of its exterior war:

Saturday evenings taken for receptions;

Sundays scorned as *popular*;

Lent invaded by the *steeple-chase*;

Holy days by shopping;

The greatest solemnities taken up with the races.

Look at it in your circle:

Always at war,

Either by declamations or smiles;

Either with the sword or the prick of a pin.

Hear it speak:

Of humility,

Of mortification,

Of resignation in the time of trial,

Of bearing outrages,

Of nobility of conduct,

Of the splendours of vanity,

Of the distinction of birth,

Of riches and pleasures.

It is in everything and everywhere, in its smallest customs, in its manner, in its laugh, or in its irritation, always opposed to the spirit, to the maxims, to the virtues of the Gospel.

This world you *cannot* love.

III.

YOU HAVE EVERY REASON NOT TO LOVE THE WORLD.

1st. First, because in not loving the world, you will not be deprived, on that account, of going in it.

You will go through domestic necessity, through family duty, through position of rank or place, through the demands of society.

2nd. If you go in it without love, you will go without danger, without illusion, without allurements, without sowing a harvest in tears, which desolates so many lives.

You will go with moderation, with disenchantment of its vanity; with that nobility which obliges, with fortune prudently spent, and will appear all the more important, and more worthy in it. Alas! must I tell you. You will appear all the more amiable and more courted in it!

3d. Finally, here is the acme: in going into the world, without loving it, you gain a thousand times more than you lose.

Alas! I should blush, humiliate myself, ask your pardon for mixing the Gospel with such sadly worldly motives; I speak humanly: "I am become foolish, you have compelled me."[1]

1. A woman who loves the world has her *mind falsified*.

She places the greatest importance on the most childish trifles; the frivolous seems the essential thing in life to her; all the qualities of the mind and heart are summed up for her in the style of a dress, and she judges of personal value by the merit of a seamstress. A life of coquetry, idleness, frivolity, vanity, egoism, sensuality, and comfort, seems to her the only life understood and conceived. She values individuals for what they possess, and what they spend.

After habituating herself to this vision, how can a woman expect to be religious in her home, in her

[1] II Cor., XII, 11.

family, in the education of her children, in her relations of society, in her reading, in her tastes, or even in her duties? A false mind, a small person with whom it is impossible to reason.

2. A woman who loves the world has her *heart weakened* and . . . . *contaminated*; trifles are her idol, success her God; and the most desired successes in the world always cost very dear; envy makes you pay for them with tears, and they are always deplorable, even when we are not obliged to shed tears over them. See, on the contrary, the woman who does not love the world, who uses the world as not using it; her heart is free and happy. She is faithful and incorruptible; in her real element of happiness, the world for her is nothing more than a ray of diversion; she escapes from cruel jealousy by her modesty; and if she has any sacrifices to make, they are richly crowned by an aureole of dignity, esteem, respect and consideration full of confidence.

3. The love of the world destroys, or at least distorts, the *grace* and *charm* of exterior *beauty*.

Must we sink to such arguments!! but at least they will make an impression on you, Ladies.

You, no *doubt*, form a false and incomplete idea of *beauty*.

Without doubt, beauty consists, in its *original type*, in that purity of lines, which the hand of the Creator delicately traced on the face of man. But the degradation of these lines is slow and steady, until it reaches the state next to ugliness or deformity; at any rate, this typical beauty is the beauty of statues.

Beauty does not know how to concede to art, adjustments destined to raise her, or rather to dissimulate her defects; that would be the fantastic and arbitrary beauty of the coloured models, which one finds in the periodical fashion books.

Imagine the most beautiful statue, ornamented and decked with all the science of fashion, with all those cares which the Latins so justly called the world, and the universe of women, *mundus muliebris*; we should have no real beauty, with its charm and its grace, without the reflection of the soul coming to illumine the human face.

Beauty, then, consists, before and above all, in the just reflex of the soul on the features, in that reflex which comes to illumine an intelligent and sweet fire in the eyes, to spread kindness and affability on the lips, to give to the whole that inexplicable graciousness which makes one forget the lines, covered as they are with the rich colours of modesty and kindness.

If, with the most regular features and the most scientific costume, the soul reflects nothing, we have insipidity; if the soul reflects arrogance in the expression, disdain on the mouth, pride and egoism in all the physiognomy, we have repulsion and disgust.

If, with features much less regular, sometimes deformed to a certain extent, and extreme simplicity in dress, the soul reflects quick intelligence, real amiability, unfeigned modesty, forgetfulness of self without calculation, goodness which tempers all, we have a graciousness which sweeps over features more than ordinary, and the grace of the colouring makes one forget entirely, the imperfection of the design.

It is true, then, that *beauty is in the soul*, and that the face is only the seat of honour where it comes to communicate with man.

So it is on this true principle that I maintain, that a woman enamoured of the world, disfigures the exterior advantages to which she clings so much and too much.

Preoccupied with a thousand frivolities, the fold and sheen of a stuff, the sparkle of a jewel, absorbed in it as in an idol, preoccupied with the effect she produces, the success she covets, she distorts her waist, her pose, her expression, and even her voice. When she wishes to be amiable and make herself interesting, she deforms her eye, contracts her mouth, her smile is perpetual (and in consequence silly) in order to show what she knows. There is nothing natural, easy, true, or dignified about her. She becomes stiff, affected, always false, even if she does not go so far as to make herself completely ridiculous.

All this game of mimic makes one portion of the human race laugh, and excites the disparagement and envy of the other portion, which knows at a glance, how to analyze all these efforts of worldly pretensions.

If being more clever, and giving herself less up to it, she wishes only to form the exterior of it, to make her soul play a borrowed rôle on the stage of the physiognomy, she will succeed no better.

It will be in vain, in the sole interest of her successes better calculated, for her to replace simplicity by coquetry, modesty by refinement of self-love; to feign in action a sweetness which she has not—a forgetfulness of self, when she is all absorbed in self; a benevolence which is only egoism, to even lavish praises which distort the face, because the success of others gnaws at her heart; she will not be able to reflect on her face the beauty which comes from the soul, because her soul is absorbed with the love of the world, and she will remember that beauty is defined as the *splendour of the true*, that *nothing is beautiful but the true*, and that the *true alone is amiable*.

On the contrary, take from a heart the love of the world, that is, the love of self within and the love of frivolity without, and you will have natural ease, dignity, grace, charm; you will have all that draws souls nobly: "Simple and natural grace shining in a glory of modesty and beauty."

Do not love the world, then, Ladies; it is to your interest as well as your duty not to do so.

In the time of St. Augustine, the Donatists separated from the Church by schism, took possession of the episcopal sees, and lead the people into errors most prejudicial to salvation.

To remedy such a great evil, St. Augustine called a council, of which he was the soul, and invited the Donatist bishops to join it, in order to persuade them to withdraw and leave the flock to their true pastors; he could obtain nothing, pride and cupidity kept them riveted to the churches which they had usurped.

Then, St. Augustine, making a supreme effort, issued this proposition in the name of all the council: " We only ask one grace of you, that you enter into unity, in order that the flock of Jesus Christ may not perish in your hands. If you will enter the bosom of the Church, we, legitimate and Catholic bishops, will come down from our episcopal pulpits and give them to you; you will retain your sees, *you will lose only your errors.*"

In another sense, Ladies, I, in finishing, address the same proposition to you, and I am being very generous towards you.

You can go into the world, provided you go without the love of the world.

In renouncing this fatal love, which is *your* enemy as well as the enemy of God, you will reserve your places in society, your superiority, and will have greater and more merited success.

You will only lose what is *ridiculous*, that which destroys grace in you, that *grace* which the Lord has made your ornament.

THE PLEASURES OF THE WORLD.

> *Nolite diligere mundum, neque ea quae in mundo sunt.*
> "Love not the world nor the things which are in the world." I John, II, 15

AFTER having seriously and thoroughly cleared the ground of the heart, in giving full force and elasticity to the word of God, by causing the anathema carried against the abuse of graces to be feared;

After having placed in the soul a solid foundation, the love of preference which we owe to God, and the destruction of the love of the world, as the secret enemy of divine love, there still remains something to do before building: it is to see that this double foundation is well placed and equally balanced.

But it will lack this balance and the edifice will threaten to sink, sometimes to fall, if, even while not loving the spirit, the maxims, and the anti-evangelical customs of the world, we allow ourselves to be stunned and intoxicated by its pleasures; if, while using moderately and christianly the pleasures of the world, we fall into the bad use of riches, into the forgetfulness of the duties which the Gospel imposes on the rich.

These, then, are the two subjects which we have yet to treat of, before putting stone on stone: the flight of the pleasures of the world, and the duties of the rich.

I understand: that if the love of the world and of all that is in the world were entirely dead in your hearts, there would be no rules to prescribe, no sacrifices to demand, divine love would have banished them all. "Love and do what you will." [1]

However, there is a corner of the heart wherein, when searched, the love of the world will still be found to cling; there it shrinks, reduces itself *to the love of the pleasures of the world*, and because we must have some pleasures, some diversions, because we think we are participating legitimately, without having the spirit of the world, we hope to escape the condemnation given in a general way.

[1] St. Augustine.

I am filling, then, a painful mission, Ladies, in speaking against your pleasures. It is a poor little stone that I have placed in the torrent that carries everything with it, and that rolls the most pious hearts pell-mell along with the most worldly and dissipated ones.

Do you see that christian who has received Jesus Christ this morning, and who receives Him very frequently; do you see her? She whirls in your circles with the same spirit, the same vivacity (and the expression is indulgent) as the lightest woman of the world who scarcely makes her Easter. And the ignoble name of the final vortex draws both the pious woman, and the one who is frankly not at all so, into the same pit.

They have reached the point of finding this very simple, of making it, they say, a preservative against dangers, a counter-balance against the excess of dissipation! Certainly, I respect all imposing decision, all enlightened direction; God grant that I may not abandon myself to rigorism, which destroys all,—but what I do know is, that the world itself is astonished at it, and that it has not yet been able to habituate itself to this mixture of communions in the morning and wild dissipation in the evening.

Here I wish to cure, not to wound; to convert, not to shock anyone. I am not ignorant of the fact that the advice for to-day will be *perfectly useless*. The world, *which laughs at everything*, will see in it the folly of a man who tries to stop the wind; and that piety *which accommodates itself to everything*, will only get out of it a discussion, which it takes upon itself to decide, will do everything just as it did before; *theological* devotion will decide the matter and say that such severity is wrong, that such sermons are too hard and should not be allowed. But it is often of necessity for the holy word to insist with importunity in season, and in an opportune way; and the scandal here is so signalized by the world itself, that the world in its turn will be scandalized at our weakness if we are silent.

Only, on such a subject, it is necessary to keep the most perfect bounds in order not to spoil the cause; the enemy is on guard, ready to parry every move, to profit by every false step, and this enemy, Ladies, is you.

I.

Let us first prove one fact which we cannot deny, that is, the *weakening and lowering of christian customs*; there is a certain practical indifference, which *accepts* everything, and never has the tyranny of fashion found more docile or obliging subjects.

"Save me, O Lord," said David, "for there is now no saint: truths are decayed from among the children of men.. They have spoken vain things, everyone to his neighbour: *with* deceitful lips and with a double heart have they spoken." [1]

To-day, it is just the contrary: with this diminution of truths, and this languishing of christian habits, they make saints at cheap rates, because it is considered that there is nothing to do to reach the holiness of a christian vocation.

This general weakening is the result of the many years, when money, success at any price, and material enjoyment, have been *everything*.

Sunday is reduced to its simplest expression;

[1] Psalm XI, 1.

The seriousness of abstinence has recriminations without end;

Lenten penance only changes and varies pleasures;

Matrimony is a matter of money above all else;

Education, a work of concessions and weaknesses;

Instruction, an exercise in leaping to scale the barrier;

Nobility, the privilege of doing nothing, and of enjoying oneself;

Alms, often the price of a ticket for a ball or a concert;

Dress, a nudity at which even the world laughs or complains;

The dance has made appalling advances in the last twenty-five years;

Piety heaps up exercises without troubling itself about virtues;

There, is the weakening of christian customs, which you cannot deny.

And this general weakening leads to not being astonished at anything, to accepting everything as soon as usage sanctions it, and prepares the way.

Twenty-five years ago, a young girl, a young wife, did not waltz, notwithstanding that the waltz was less rapid; to-day a mother becomes ridiculous, exaggerated in the eyes of the world, even in the eyes of her children, if she restrains her daughter, and everything flags in worldly circles if they dance with a certain restraint, instead of whirling around out of measure.

DUTIES OF THE RICH.

Divitibus hujus saeculi praecipe non superbi sapere
"Charge the rich of this world not to be high-minded" Tim., vi, 17

THE holy use of riches, with the flight of the pleasures of the world, is going to achieve, to consolidate, and place the foundation of a christian life.

Charge the rich of this world not be high-minded, consequently to be simple in their tastes.

St. Paul, in teaching Timothy, and tracing out for him the *duties* which he should recall to the rich, gave the first place to the rigorous duty of *simplicity in taste*; then came, in order, the duty, of indifference for the uncertain goods which they possessed, of pious works, and, finally, of alms.

Notwithstanding this lesson, we always speak to the rich of mercy and charity; it is the unique theme addressed to them.

This method upsets the order fixed by the apostle; displaces and mutilates the duties.

In speaking only of alms, we give the rich an *incorrect* thought; that of thinking themselves providences or necessary wheels to providential action. It leads them to think that they have little need to be charitable for their own sakes, and always makes mean benefactors of them, when they should be formed on a broad and christian line.

If this flattering method obtains the immediate end of gaining a large receipt for the poor, it misses the superior end, of indicating to the rich, the best means of salvation for themselves.

For, in the words of the apostle, it is question not of a counsel, but of a rigorous command, *praecipe*, not of an arbitrary order, which placed the words as they came from the pen, but of a chain of ideas, the rings of which being *soldered* by the Holy Ghost.

In establishing simplicity of thought and taste in all conduct as the *first* duty of the chain, there is only one objection to be feared :

That is, that alms will supply all, fill all voids, repair all faults, acquit all responsibility, and at the supreme judgment, will be the one motive, the one consideration in a favourable sentence.

But as the rich shall one day enter heaven, by the power alone of alms, because alms shall have merited for them here below all expiation and all grace; so alms shall have merited simplicity for them before all else, which is its first duty.

On earth, alms make the rich simple and penitent, as in heaven they shall make them happy forever.

The foundation, then, of all the duties for the rich, is simplicity of thought, feeling, and taste. It is this simplicity which makes them tremble at the uncertainty of fortune, ambition more solid goods, establish the real foundation of the christian life, and spread alms with facility. This is the attitude above all which rich christians must acquire, leaving the pride of life to the rich of the world.

The pride of life produces the greatest disorder with the rich, and by pride I do not mean those haughty manners, which one avoids simply because they are bad form, because they savour of wealth and expose one to ridicule or hatred, and would serve our civilized self-love very badly.

I mean that vain glory which wealth nearly always produces in the heart, even though one covers it with a false varnish, more likely to preserve, than to destroy it.

I.

SIMPLICITY OF THE RICH TOWARDS THEMSELVES.

Out of the abundance of the gifts of the earth, it is difficult even for the best of us to persuade ourselves that this fortune is not our due, that it is not perfectly simple and natural for us to possess it.

If fortune comes from birth and ancestors, we are acclimated from infancy to this atmosphere of wellbeing, never having breathed any other air, so that we cannot even imagine that things might have been otherwise.

If fortune comes from work, activity, ability, intelligence and success in life, it is still more difficult for us not to think it our just right, and that it is only just that we should enjoy the fruits of our labours.

This disorder of the mind produces two false and disastrous ideas:

1st. It makes the former class forget that it did not depend upon them, but upon the will and goodness of God alone, that they were born under such conditions; and the latter, that industry, activity and intelligence are the pure gifts of God, that successes were managed by Providence, that to annihilate all, it would have been sufficient to impair the health, or interfere with time, and a chain of providential cares was necessary for them to amass their fortune.

2nd. It exaggerates the nature and essence of proprietorship — Proprietorship! this word *which fills the mouth*, implies at once the idea of something so much our own, that we hold it only from ourselves, without any account to render, any duty to fill, or any responsibility to carry. False idea, for proprietorship has two ends, one to earth and one to heaven. With regard to earth, proprietorship is an inviolable right, placed under the guarantee of society and the protection of laws, but with regard to God, the sovereign master, it is nothing more than a temporary use which God has burdened with payments, the lease of which he breaks at His wish, and of which He asks a most rigorous account at death. Before men, we are proprietors; before God we are tenants, and if we wish to consider things in their true light, we shall see that actual ownership is only a word, and that if we have the advantage or rather the *disadvantage* over the ordinary user of being able to transfer, to change the property, it is after all, only a temporary use on a larger and sadder scale. Besides it is we who reduce proprietorship to its strictest use.

We lessen the enjoyment of it by thinking only of acquiring, of preserving and enlarging it for our children or for an uncertain future; thus from hand to hand, and generation to generation, the proprietorship rolls, without leaving its size and abundance even to the entail, and if careless ancestors use it freely, we think that they have taken too large a share of the temporary loan.

The simple rich will have just ideas, because they will have christian ones, they will not be elated by goods which they have received from the pure bounty of God, and their gratitude will be very humble, because they will know that they have not merited so many favours, that often they have merited them less, than those on whom God has not bestowed them.

They will then use the world as not using it, they will possess as not possessing and you will see the portrait of the rich traced by St. Augustine, forming in their hearts.

"There are those who are in opulence and honour during time who do not put their hope either in their lands, their money, or in passing honours; but place their confidence more securely in the real Good; they acquire nothing by succession, they lose nothing by death. They seem to have a great deal of the goods of this world, but are so detached in heart and conduct, and make such a merciful use of it, that they deserve to be counted among the poor of the Gospel. They see that this world is full of uncertainty and perils, that we are truly strangers and travellers in this land, and conduct themselves in their possessions as in an Inn; they pass through the use of wealth without possessing it or being possessed by it; they gather pleasure in passing, but do not bind themselves to it as though never to be separated from it."

II.

SIMPLICITY OF THE RICH TOWARDS THEIR NEIGHBOUR.

A second disorder of the pride of riches is to think oneself of a different nature from those who do not possess a fortune, and to scorn them.

Do not be frightened, thinking that I am giving up the rich to the irritation of the poor classes. I am speaking only of the rich who are not made humble by their religion; we should also have a great deal to say about the pride of the poor with regard to the rich, and the inferior classes are less irritated when the christian pulpit does justice to all. Truth always calms hearts, while passion (or lack of moderation), serves but to sour and revolt them.

Yes, the pride of riches after having given us a false idea of our personal value, and of the nature of the goods we possess, corrupts even the esteem we should have for our fellow creatures, and inclines us to look upon them as being of another nature from ourselves, made of a coarser clay, or at least as not having cast off a coat which makes them differ essentially.

1st. The forms of education, politeness, good breeding, distinguished manners, urbanity of language, and even material habits in the life of ease, make such a contrast with the lack of education, coarse manners, rudeness, unpolished language, that it is difficult not to allow all this difference from without, to effect, through our mind, the depths of our nature.

Let us speak plainly : it is difficult to think that a hard hand which is habitually dirty, is of the same flesh and blood as the hand cared for with excess and kept in the shade of a delicate prism. Easy error, which goes further than we think, and which has caused it to be said with truth, that the crime committed by a coarse hand armed with a rough instrument, excites no other interest than to see in it the affair of the hangman. But the crime, in straw coloured gloves or gray, the colour matters but little, however refined it may be, if it has mixed the poison with a delicate white hand, leaves after it a perfume of dramatic poetry which excites the attention of the most honest hearts, and often becomes of great interest to the public.

Without going to this excess, which is not chimerical, I say that it is necessary for the rich to have the full weight of humility in order to restrain the false judgments of pride; to say thoroughly to themselves: that they owe the varnish of education to God; that the absence of this varnish does not alter our nature which is the same in all; that often under this coarse exterior, there is an upright, excellent heart, a pure generous soul, and sometimes heroic virtues which are not always to be found under the most brilliant exteriors.

Pride easily leads us to think that our fellow creatures are not of the same species as ourselves. Christian simplicity in wealth will always reëstablish the level of God, or will even lower it, to the extent of humiliating us with a guilty inferiority, if the most precious gifts of heaven do not end in making us more imperfect and more ungrateful.

If the rich do not give themselves a large share of humility, not only the goods of the soul and its culture, but the most material goods, those the most foreign to their personal value, will make them entertain this false judgment, which classes men as God has not classed them.

Is it not true, Ladies, that while scarcely being conscious of it, we think ourselves extensive like our property, great like our dwellings, sumptuous like our tables, valuable like our clothes, distinguished like our decorations and our insignia? If we are well served, we imagine by instinct that it should be so, delicate food seems to suit our innate appetites; the richness of materials seems to have been woven and made for us; and the society which surrounds us, engrossed with the science and the talent by which it may flatter us, is only a nimbus, which should shine naturally around our heads, so inclined are we to identify ourselves with all foreign worth!

For, if this vain glory is not suppressed and constrained, how easy it is to think oneself as something apart,—and what work of humility is necessary in order to note the merit of each one by the honesty of the heart and the dignity of conduct alone.

3d. Profound wisdom of my God! With simplicity of feeling, you have made the charm which soothes the irritation made by the inequality of fortune.

You rich of the world! do not wait for those forced reconciliations, which make you take the hand of *everyone* at the moment when the social tempest is ready to engulf you. Know that the poor curse the bread you give them, if you do not give them at the same time that honor which they can merit by resignation in a laborious life; that the workman is irritated with pay for his work, if you do not give some homage of confidence and consideration to his uprightness and devotion with it, and that all would bravely bear inferiority if those who command and enjoy life would soften it by christianly humble relations.

There is only one step from this feeling of vain glory, which places us in another category from the rest of mankind, to the scorn of those whom Providence has deprived of, or favoured less with the gifts of fortune.

By scorn as by pride; again it is not question of disdainful and insulting manners which education corrects,—and this education is due, above all, to the christian atmosphere breathed since our infancy into those customs, which seem natural to us, and which we owe to the Gospel. To scorn is to *under prize*, not to estimate a thing at its true value.

Then, do not judge the rich by your heart, which is christian in its fortune, judge them under the sole influence of what fortune in itself inspires.

For wealth, if it is not possessed with simplicity of feeling, carries with it the instinct of contempt for those who do not possess it.

1st. "Brethren," said St. James, "if there shall come into your assembly a man having a golden ring, in fine apparel, and there shall come in also a poor man in mean attire. And you have respect to him that is clothed with the fine apparel, and shall say to him: Sit thou here well, but say to the poor man, stand thou there or sit under my footstool: Do you not judge within yourselves, and are become judges of unjust thoughts?"[1]

Those excesses seem very far from our customs. Do you know why? it is because, for eighteen centuries, this word of St. James has purified the world in crossing it; it is because, for eighteen centuries, the Gospel has been working at the edu-

[1] James, II, 2, 3, 4.

cation and civilization of man, and because we gather, unconsciously, the fruit of this imperceptible work.

But see how many disorders still remain.

The poor are not humiliated, because means have been found in the rules of social relations not to expose them to humiliation, by never encountering them. They are avoided even on those sacred days which God made partly to bring all classes together; on these days it is good form to avoid the poor classes, and to affect a neglected attire, in order not to compromise oneself by resembling them even at a great distance; in this the spirit of the world has found the means of guarding our pride, of taking from Sunday its reverential costumes, and of giving us one more folly, all at the same time.

By honouring fortune for the sake of fortune, no matter what its source or use, you scorn mediocrity in consequence.

Tell me, you rich of the world, if in your reunions you forbid that opulence which has been acquired with the saddest suspicions? Tell me if your functions receive those of doubtful reputations with coldness when they are covered with gold; if you do not seek to be admitted there yourselves, where all is wiped out before that wealth which makes a great show, which offers you entertainment, which governs the world, or has the privilege of a deplorable celebrity? Tell me if, in the most approved language (and it is only thus consecrated, because it is the faithful expression of custom), there are not those stereotyped phrases which accuse, under the cover of good form, the unjust distance which the haughty heart puts between the children of God? Now, not counting them in *society*, properly speaking; now, not according them even *that entrance into life*, which is the same for all; now, refusing to age, science, merit, the smallest appellation of honour to lavish it with affectation there, where familiarity should naturally suppress it?

Ah! how far we are from that rule of the holy scriptures which gives contempt to the wicked and unjust, and reserves *all respect* for those who fear the Lord!

How far we are from that moral of St. Gregory, who tells us never to honour in men the goods of this world, but only the image of God, to which they were created.

Give it up! give it up! simplicity of feeling and tastes will not displace any fortune, change any rank, nor disturb the harmony of any social relation; but it will calm the world, console inferiority, and make all superiority acceptable and respected.

2nd. This disdain for our brother produces still another disorder, of which I shall only say a word:

It is, that we think we have always done too much for others, who seem so inferior to us, and never enough for ourselves.

Do not reassure yourselves on certain alms which you must give after all, and of which we will neither weigh the motive nor the measure here. Go down into your heart and see. Inundated with wealth, you think you have done great things when you have given a little bread, and complain that they are always asking! Having great power, you think you have well paid the most devoted services by the slightest protection, and complain that they are never content. You give the least possible of your influence and superiority, and imagine that you have loaded them with services! The smallest remuneration goes against you; you dispute in a narrow soul a few coins which are going to pass into other hands, while your soul enlarges all at once to incredible proportions when it is question of an expensive folly which relates to yourselves!

Ah! how many wounds that simplicity, recommended by St. Paul, is charged to cure in our hearts!

SIMPLICITY OF THE RICH TOWARDS GOD.

The pride of life after having made us *egotistical* toward ourselves, *unjust* towards our neighbours, makes us ungrateful and independent towards God.

1st. If the rich of the world are struck in their turn by some of those misfortunes which weigh so heavily on all the children of Adam! If they are not irritated they are astonished, thinking themselves, even unconsciously, of a different species from the rest of humanity. They cannot understand how, in all their abundance of material goods, with a dwelling more than healthy, with food more than choice, with attentions from which nothing is spared, misfortune can come to knock at their door; for them it is an enigma of self-love, and they will sometimes explain it to themselves with such naïve egoism, that it is necessary to have heard the expressions to believe them. They do not understand this word of Tobias: "If we have received benefits from the hand of the Lord, why should we not receive misfortunes from It?" They do not understand that word of St. Peter: "Whom resist, ye, strong in faith, knowing that the same affliction befalls your brethren who are in the world."[1]

The humble rich man will draw greater patience, and a more noble resignation from the grateful thought of the goods with which he is inundated; in the sight of the miseries which weigh on men so universally, he will say to himself that he is still spared, cared for while so many others want. But the haughty rich man only thinks in a vague way of this suffering of others; cared for to excess in a sickness, he will never think that there are thousands of others worse than he is, who are deprived of care; to the poor who abandon themselves to idleness, he will readily say with St. Paul: "If any man will not work, neither let him eat;"[2] and will think that he has the right to seat himself at a sumptuous table while leading a perfectly useless

[1] I Peter, v, 9.   [2] II Thess., III, 10.

life, refusing to work in his way for the public good!

2nd. The rich man of the world will never think of raising his heart to God with humble feelings, of judging himself unworthy of so many favours, or of being grateful for so much bounty. He will enjoy all, will abuse all, as though he had an inviolable right to it, as though he had merited this providential preference; as though it were simple and natural that he should have found, in appearing on earth, this endowment, this lion's share of the children of God.

On the contrary, the humble rich christian doubles his joy by the feeling of gratitude; not a gift of nature comes to him but he says to himself that thousands of others are more worthy, and humbly blesses Providence, which has given him beyond his merits and his aspirations.

If, in the middle of the rigorous season, a bright hearth cheers his heart; if his family are warmed by eiderdown and furs, he thinks of his brothers, scarcely protected from the killing excesses of the cold. If his commodious house is sheltered from the least wind, he thinks of the thousands of houses where the cold wind enters and whistles through so many openings. If he seats himself at a delicately served table, it is not without raising his eyes to heaven, and lowering his heart towards so many, for whom coarse bread is scarce and uncertain. If, in summer, he is shaded from the heat of the day, in a large airy house; if he goes to breathe the fresh air under the shade of trees, his thoughts revert to his fellow-creatures, who carry the weight of the day and the heat while working in the fields. If he throws himself on a soft bed, he thinks of the great number of cots badly placed for fresh air or against the cold. If he is stretched on a sick bed, he blesses God for having multiplied the most attentive and delicate attentions around him. Finally, if in the affairs of life he sees himself served with zeal and devotion, he draws the conclusion from it, that he should show himself the most faithful and devoted servant of God.

That is what simplicity in the rich produces ; pride and haughty tastes will only inspire him with ingratitude and insensibility.

But here is the last disorder, and perhaps the greatest one, or at least the source of all the others, it is that the pride of wealth causes a sad independence towards God.

1st. The great end of religion, of the link of man with God, is to place us under the humble dependence of the sovereign Master. It is for this reason that God and the Church, which is His organ, exacts periodical dependencies of liberty, time, fortune and even food. It is necessary that man, held at a distance from evil and drawn towards good, should still be made to feel, by exterior precepts, that his liberty has a master, that time is not his own, that his wealth is burdened, that his life even, which he sustains by food, is a thread placed in the hands of God.

God wishes that this dependence, which weighs so heavily on the poor, whose existence is as uncertain as the birds; on the workman, who owes his time and his strength to his employer; on the merchant, who scarcely ever enjoys a moment of leisure; on the public man, all of whose time belongs to those who claim his ministry or care, should also weigh on the rich, with whom liberty is almost without bounds, and that if his social position exempts him from a number of painful duties, he should consecrate his life generously to the use of all, and consider himself, in the sight of God, placed under the yoke of a more exemplary fidelity.

Listen to this lamentable word of Jeremiah: "Go about through the streets of Jerusalem and see, and consider, and seek in the broad places thereof, if you can find a man that executeth judgment, and seeketh faith. . . . . But I said, perhaps these are poor and foolish, that know not the way of the Lord, the judgment of their God. I will go therefore to the great men, and will speak to them, for they have known the way of the Lord, the judgment of their God. And behold, these have already broken the yoke more, and have burst the bonds."[1]

Ladies, is not this your portrait: is it not among the rich, religious in appearance, that we find more inclination and ardour to escape from the dependence of God? Is it not in the midst of opulence, when it is not profoundly sanctified by humility, that we see in action this system of doing as little as possible for God, when through justice and gratitude we should do more? Is it not they, who are continually in search, on foot, or perpetually question-

[1] Jeremiah, v, 1, 4, 5.

ing to know what they are not obliged to do, and of what they can be dispensed?

Sometimes we counsel you to deduct from your income a *portion* for the poor, as a liege, homage, and payment to the sovereign domain of God, and this advice has found a thousand objections, not through avarice or severity, you give often as much and more, but because this christian measure attacks liberty in its *principle*, and establishes a dependence which you do not want.

Do you hear those cries against the least inconvenience, those incessant complaints against penitential abstinences, those murmurs against a law which is not understood, which they want to shake off; those desires which call for the lessening of the precepts; that joy which resounds when they hear it is modified? From whence come these clamours? From the poor and the little ones, for whom all is privation? Rarely, Ladies, when these little ones, these poor, are christians.

This horror of all constraint is formulated by the rich, who call themselves religious; by the rich, for whom art succeeds in eluding nearly all penance, who scarcely refuse anything to superabundant sensuality, whose table, around which so much murmuring clatters, would be a feast for the two-thirds of men even on a fast day! I do not wish to attack this luxury and these habits of ease; they can have their use in the world; but I do not think I am exacting too much in asking that a little inconvenience, a little penance, should be received with more respect and submission.

2nd. Independence towards God, born of ingratitude of the heart and the corruption of wealth, defends itself badly in doing only the least possible for God. It pretends not to do anyone any harm, but it deceives itself. Violation of a right is a harm, and God, who is *some one*, has a right to our dependence. You close yourselves within the limits of the strictest obligations when it is question of religion; but if God acted thus towards you, where would you be? He owes you a little bread to sustain life; He has given only that to a great many others as worthy as you; see what He has added to your daily bread! He owes you the most simple, coarsest material for clothing to protect you from the inclemencies of the weather; He owes you a little house to live in, a little field to get your existence from ; He has not given more to the larger number of men ; calculate now what He has added to your sumptuous clothes, your commodious houses, your vast estates !

Ah ! are you not obliged, on this account, to draw all the more gratitude and submission from a holy simplicity ?

In indicating, Ladies, all these disorders, that spring from the pride of life, please God it was not my wish to pour bitterness or irritation on the wealthy class. The wealthy can be simple, submissive, and merciful ; the poor, haughty, spiteful, and unsubmissive. I have only wished to speak of the faults which wealth draws in its wake, when it is not guarded from corruption by humility. I have wished to tell the rich of the world that they deceive themselves when they are only charitable ; that their first duty is to be humble ; that it is from this principal duty that all the other virtues spring, and to depend but little on the uncertainty of the goods of this world, to put the foundation of all their hope in God, to become rich in the fruits of salvation.

Above all, I have wished to tell them, that humility is the abundant source of all mercy. Give us, in reality, rich who are persuaded that their fortune is a pure gift of God, that their lands are burdened with a rigorous responsibility, that they should consider men as their brothers, see in them only the image of God; finally, that they should hold themselves in a continual state of gratitude and dependence under the hand of God; give us, I say, such rich, and at a word we can make more worthy, more christian, more delicate, and more abundant alms flow from their hearts, than we could by all the discourses, which excite a passing sensibility, or the emotion of personal interest.

Finally, I have wished to say, that St. Paul, in instructing the rich of the world, had many reasons for placing at the head of their duties simplicity of tastes, *non superbe sapere*; and at the end, like the stream below its source, the facility of giving, the noble ease of charity.

PORTRAIT OF THE CHRISTIAN WOMAN.

Mulierem fortem quis inveniet.
"Who shall find a valiant woman."
Prov., xxxi, 10.

THIS question, which the Sage puts to himself, in the book of Proverbs, and seems to propose as an enigma, is very sad for you, Ladies.

It is true that if the Sage had wished to return the question, and had asked, who shall find a valiant man, valiant in the duties of each day, courageous in the ordinary difficulties of life, who makes himself worthy of the name of man by a useful, devoted life, nobly occupied and nobly laborious, he would have been obliged to put the question in a more humiliating manner still. The Sage responds that we must look far for the valiant woman, that her price is rare and high, like the things that come from the extremities of the earth.

However, I wish to show you to-day, Ladies, that it is not necessary to hunt the ends of the earth for this valiant woman, that she is probably in your midst, and after having placed and consolidated the true foundations of a christian life, perhaps you will be very glad to see them vivified by action.

Come, then, and see a christian woman *at work;* come and see how she gives her hands to useful things.

I shall not take her in the *whole* of her life, in her duties towards God, which have the preference of her heart, and inspire her with a piety that is neither ridiculous, disagreeable, nor troublesome; in her duties towards her neighbour, whom she embalms with sweetness and charity; or in her duties towards herself, which always give to her conduct a suave and even dignity, that would be great, and besides the discussion is not established on *all the surface* of this ground.

I take her, in her contact with her family and the world, with its usages and its diversions, and I place her, *this christian,* on that inclined plane where your feet waver, on that springing-board, from which you bound to throw yourselves into the world.

Here is my christian, that is to say, *the christian of the Gospel* and of baptismal engagements.

1st. I acknowledge from the start, that she is not what is so cheaply styled *a saint* . . . . she is simply a . . . . good christian.

She laughs at these modern inventions of reduced rates of *canonization*, and of sanctity by the quantity, which makes heroism of virtues accessible to all and justifies by acclamation our mean outlay towards God.

She is not placed in shining exceptions for works. She is neither a Boilet, a Longueville, a Chantal, nor an Avrillot de Champlatreux.

See: she is a person like you, has your name, lives your life, sees the world that you see. Like you, she has a husband, a family, relations, duties, sorrows. Like you, she has faults, miseries to correct; but she does not love them, she does not canonize them, she humiliates herself by them, and corrects them by constant work. We perceive this victory over self at each Communion, and those who surround and serve her, seeing her greater efforts on these days, her more contained gentleness, her serenity, which pierces through and drives away all clouds, say to themselves: *She has received Holy Communion to-day.* It is thus that they guess her communion days. It is a means of knowing that she deserves another.

In brief: she tends to sanctity, and will reach heaven; while waiting, she is content to be frankly christian to reach it, to draw virtues from her religious exercises, to walk at a distance in the steps of the saints.

Imitate her, Ladies; be a little less of a saint according to the world, and a little more of a *christian* according to the Gospel.

2nd. My christian has been reared by a pious and worthy mother, for it is rare that we gather grapes from thorns, and figs from brambles; such productions are exceptions and miracles of grace.

From her earliest infancy, her mother has placed two *fruitful germs* in her heart; like Blanche, she taught her to prefer God to all, and as a result, she taught her to overcome self. Love of God *above* all things, abnegation of self *in* all things, small or great, that is the only real education, the only one that influences all our life, the only one that forms noble hearts, *elevated* souls (it is the name given to education,—we say a person has or has not been raised), the only one, in fact, that produces valiant women and men worthy of the name.

With these principles, and in proportion as age advanced, this mother avoided two *faults* in education—that of making her child *her idol*, and of teaching her *to pose as an idol*.

Let me explain myself: to make an idol of one's daughter, is to see in her only perfections, ravishing beauty, exquisite style, brilliant wit, charming character, even in her sulky, headstrong moods; it is to spoil one's children (to *spoil* them!) to flatter and idolize them without ever correcting a single fault in them.

To teach one's daughter to make an idol of herself is, in infancy, not to give her any other recompense or punishment than that of dress (you shall have, or you shall put on a pretty gown), and when she is grown, it is to insinuate to her that everything is due to woman, that she has only to command, to govern, to reign in the first places, and take a decided cutting air; and to misrepresent sadly to her the consideration with which christian society respectfully surrounds woman.

These two faults are terrible; for woman is by nature a creature *of vanity*; and she is destined in the world to become a creature of *devotion*. In making her your idol, you magnify the product of her vanity; in making her play the rôle of idol, you kill her instincts of devotion. The charm of woman is in her disdain of vanity, then she is natural, simple, and gracious; the empire of woman is in her modesty, devotion, and spirit of sacrifice; virtues and strength, which those affected efforts to be amiable and make oneself interesting, will never supplant.

3d. Thus reared, my christian is now established in the world, and the virtue which dominates all others in her position of wife, is that she loves *her home*.

She loves her husband, and the life of the domestic hearth is not simply a juxtaposition, where you see each other at meals and for a few moments when you do not know what to do, or have nothing to say; it is a union of heart and not an obliged encounter; a happy mingling of thoughts, projects, counsels, and not a household where each one pulls in his own way.

She loves her children, whom she rears,—remark I do not say that she instructs them, she rears them,—she presides actually over their education, and places with love those solid foundations on which high thought, exalted feeling, sensibility of heart, and nobility of conduct, are to be established, and true religion founded on practical abnegation.

She loves *her duties*, in spite of their simplicity, monotony, and severity. It is her sphere, and all that shines outside of that is for her only relaxation, social decorum or christian charity.

It is not necessary for her to expand herself outside in order to breathe and to live, as if the conjugal atmosphere was too rarified in one sense, too heavy in another; she would content herself perfectly with her home life, if duty did not call her out of it.

They tell us, Ladies, there is an Academy, called the Academy of Silence. This literary body has also its meetings and receptions, where all passes by signs, emblems, figured actions, without uttering a single word.

One day there was question of admitting a candidate who pressed his admission very persistently;

they could not admit him, as their official number was complete; the president, to signify this, filled a vase with water with such precision that it was physically impossible to add one drop without its running over. The candidate, without getting discouraged, placed a rose leaf on the full vase, and the water did not even tremble. That was to indicate in the most ingenious manner that the complete number was not an invincible obstacle. Then the president wrote on the board the number one hundred, the sacred and insuperable number, and nothing is as severe as a cipher. The candidate modestly placed a zero before the hundred to show that his admission would not change the number; overcome by so much wit, modesty, and silence, the president put the zero after the hundred, thus proclaiming that in changing this time the sacred cipher, the Academy of a hundred, would be worth a thousand, and the candidate was received beyond the number.

Let us return to our christian; if, in presenting herself to this Academy, they proposed to her in writing this question : "What is the world to you, to a woman whose heart is attached to her hearth and her family?" She would have placed a rose leaf on a full vase.

4th. My christian then has *her heart full ;* the world for her is a rose leaf which does not trouble in any way its plenitude. She does not have merely her body at home, while her heart is roaming in dreams and extravagant suppositions.

She does not think herself either misunderstood or wretched.

She does not nourish her melancholy, or a dreamy mind with romances, which carry her far from the realities of life, the impassioned reading of which will always corrupt the mind, and weaken the heart.

If she is obliged to allow these books in her house, because she is not sole mistress, she at least takes great care that they shall not lie around on the furniture, for fear that her servants or children may come and feed themselves by stealth with this food, which is always empty and unsavoury, unless it be highly seasoned to suit the taste.

5th. This christian, who is also yours, is she not, Ladies? This christian, who is you, or at least whom you wish to imitate, *does not love the world nor the things of the world.*

Let us understand each other; she does not fly from the intercourse of society by a bizarre devotion; she finds those ties and associations which duty, form, and even a legitimate interest have rendered necessary, respectable; she goes into society for her husband, for her children's future, for whom she prepares acquaintances and helps in advance; my God! let us say all, she goes *for herself* also, yes, yes, a little on her own account; for, having nothing bitter or singular in her religion, she likes honest, christian, moderate pleasure; she uses it with sobriety, she relaxes herself—*in pleasure*, understand it well. But the pleasure which one gathers in passing is very different from *the love of pleasure*, which makes one giddy and captivates one; she does not like the world that is so often opposed to the Gospel, to morality, to the decency of dress; she does not like it in its hostility towards God, no matter what good form it may give it, or in its pretensions to make accommodations and concessions in everything, or in its false wisdom, which plays the oracle, or in that pretended authority which it assumes to decide everything.

Not loving the world, in so far as it is the enemy of Jesus Christ, she does not care at all for the *things* which are in the world, and *of the world*, that is to say, all those batteries which are set off against the maxims and virtues of the Gospel. If she likes honest *pleasure*, which one can enjoy in society, her mind being just, and her heart remaining true, she detests all that the world adds to season, after its fashion, the insipidity of pleasure; indecency, immodesty, coquetry, and levity; wickedness, malignity, rivalry, and competitions; pride, sufficiency, severity, vanity, worshipping of fortune; she does not sanction ease, sensuality, frivolity, the utterly useless life. Homage appears either very superficial or sadly interested to her; envied triumphs make her smile, since they are due to the quality of a stuff and its sheen, the art which has draped the folds, or the letters of some invitations; as for successes, she dreads them, they cost tears of bitterness, if they do not cause tears of repentance.

That which the christian woman still does not like in the world is the little respect which its diversions have for the forms of her religion, and for the limits of the penitential time. She has *her season* of pleasure.

. She does not understand that instinct of the world, which crowds its reunions in on Saturday evenings, so that the sacred morning of Sunday is wasted by the fatigue of both master and servant.

She does not comprehend those established divisions, which allow the gaieties to be continued till the middle of Lent, or at least not to give all up until then; or allows them to go on even until Passion Sunday; and if it were not for the sadness of the thing, she would laugh at the incredible penance (which, nevertheless, presumes to be very edifying), which consists in replacing balls by dinners, the play and concerts.

She is astounded when they tell her that even Holy Week would be too long, if it were not varied by some strictly *sacred concerts, by promenades*, where the fashions are set, and where oddly enough the mourning[1] of the death of a God is worn; she is afflicted when she sees the greatest, the holiest days of religion, absorbed, and the character of the day changed by the worship of the steeple-chase.

[1] In France mourning is worn during Holy Week.

But what astonishes the christian woman above all, is that the conduct of the world in all this should be accepted as an infallible rule; that there is nothing to say when the first little person who comes along tells you in a superior tone: "We are to have concerts up to a certain time"; and the world making *its rules for Lent*, according to its fancy, the law is received as an irreversible decision and much better practised than the rules of a legitimate authority.

Finally, if charity itself — charity abusing of means, and making money out of everything — should place its fêtes, declamations, and *quasi*-theatrical representations on holy days, our christian would content herself with sending an offering, so that the poor should not be deprived of it.

6th. It is with these dispositions, with her heart full of her duties, and penetrated with the vanity of the world, that the christian woman is going to appear in it.

She will not take her children in it *too soon*. She knows that the snow-drop does not need cultivation, and that vanity is a fruit which ripens soon enough. Still less will she make an *exhibition*

of her daughters when she does take them in it.
Even should she be wanting in christian feelings
and maternal dignity, she is not ignorant of the
fact that this means is out of date, that the parade
is useless, that the matter is better managed in the
dry positive *study* than in the glitter of an entertainment, that all is a question of numerals, and the
accessories will only be placed as fractions, that
beauty will add but little, the qualities of the heart
only figure for form, and that this beauty (of which
a mother is not a judge), lacking in spite of all
adornment, will only diminish the mercenary value
the more. That which occupies her rather here,
is not to allow herself to be taken with this *rôle*
which youth plays for a few hours on the stage of
the world, but to wish to know people in themselves, with their share of qualities, faults, and not
under the gracious mask which they put on for a
few moments, which sometimes hide the most egotistical and desolating character for the home.

7th. My christian dresses; she is about to start;
be attentive, Ladies.

Her husband thinks it proper that she should go
out; he has even urged her to do so. As for her,

with her moderate desires, she obeys form, and gives herself up to a certain amount of pure pleasure, which constitutes her diversion.

Do not think that she will be the least ridiculous; the world has never branded her with that hot iron, which it has ever in hand. She is neither *the first* to follow the fashions, that would be too conspicuous, *nor the last*, that would be too negligent. She bends with reserve before the exigencies of what they call, without doubt by anti-phrase, *dressing oneself;* she knows how to dress.

She will not discuss, with the measure in her hand, the length of a garment—she knows that inches do not mean much; she will not wage war with tissues more or less gauzy; and of two women similarly dressed, the one will be in the bad form of coquetry, and our christian will have the great charm of perfect appropriateness. It is because simplicity of the heart presides over all . . . . ; because she wishes to please but two persons, God and her husband; then everything arranges, plaits, and drapes itself, and when all is finished, *with promptitude*, she obtains the approbation which she ambitions—that of a wise mother, and a husband who loves and respects her.

She is ready on time, without making others wait for her (this punctuality reveals a moderation full of wisdom); but here her heart sighs, she is leaving her little children, who are already asleep. She leans over the cradle, without fearing to crumple herself, and kisses them tenderly, blesses them, and leaves them in the care of God.

Then, sustained by an arm which is dear to her, she starts, she is gone. A wise thought occupies her on her way, which will give the expression to her natural physiognomy; it is her just and exalted mind refusing to believe that she is more worthy under a fluff of lace and a tiara, than when she wears in all simplicity, her crown of wife and mother.

Our christian has arrived; listen! she is announced. She appears. A slight murmur of sweet veneration rustles and rises; this murmuring is not caused by her beauty, or by her toilet. That all exists, but it is all lost in a happy harmony, which results from a perfect decorum.

Decorum, Ladies, that is the ray relieved by shadows, which pervades every glance, and charms all the more in that it so seldom shines; it is that reflection that commands the respect of a sweet affection.

One knows at once that the woman who has just been announced is good, charitable, observing, and condescending; that she is without envy, and is frankly pleased with the success of others, all the more so in that she does not seek it for herself. One knows that all these qualities are not a part that she is playing for a few hours; that she has not two voices, one sweet before people, the other bitter in aside remarks; one caressing in society, the other harsh and imperious in her home; then, too, the murmur of approbation which receives her, the admiration which follows her steps and her movements, are as sincere as they are complete in the minds of all—both men and women.

Decidedly, I must acknowledge to you, that my christian does not waltz—it will be in vain for you to reason against it, she will not give in, and you will pardon her this firmness since all else in her is so consistent. However, she has seen the world smile, with that smile which disconcerts the strongest souls; this smile has probably touched her vanity as woman, but it has not penetrated her heart—there is no place for it there. As to grieving over it, it is impossible; she is a christian.

At the first sign she leaves, disappears. She returns home gladly, penetrated with the vanity of all that she has seen, with the futility of all that she has heard, with the misery of all these little gewgaws, from which she frees herself as soon as possible. The thought of her home and the duties which she is about to begin again, is much sweeter to her.

For our christian, without being a *saint*, leads *a regular, useful, mortified life, in union with God*, which procures more real joy for her than the dissipation of the world, followed by the disgust which discolours what is real in life.

Ladies, I have just drawn your portrait; and if you do not find it sufficiently like you, blame only the inability of my pencil.

I have given you the outline, the drawing; it is for you to develop the whole with well managed shadows, with rich and perfectly stable colours.

After having preached this sermon once, I received a note signed: "One of your hearers who wishes to be a disciple."—"A woman who wishes to be your christian."

It was the greatest praise I received. Do not take the trouble to write *to me*. . . . . Say to, and promise God, these two points: disciple and christian.

Yes, you wish it; desire it more and more; you will lose what is false, frivolous, futile, dangerous, bitter, guilty. You will gain what is true, solid, consoling, pleasing, sweet, worthy of you and your salvation.

THE REGULATED LIFE.

> *Fundamentum posui, unusquisque videat quomodo superaedificet.*
> "I have laid the foundation and another buildeth thereon But let every man take heed how he buildeth thereon " I Cor , III, 10

AFTER having dug deeply down, and thoroughly cleared away all obstacles, we placed and consolidated the foundation of the christian life; the love of preference given to God and the killing in ourselves of the love of the world.

But foundations, Ladies, are only placed in order to build on them; they call for the edifice which one desires to build; and it is here, says St. Paul, that each one should consider how to build, and how to construct, on this foundation : *Unusquisque videat quomodo superaedificet.*

What you are to build now, shall it be of gold, silver, and precious stones?

This building will resist the fire of worldly concupiscence, or the fire of the Lord's anger.

Shall it be of dry wood, hay, or stubble? These miserable materials will be destroyed and consumed by the least flame, and fire, is to be the proof of the work of each of us: *Uniuscujusque opus ignis probabit.*[1]

Do you know, Ladies, what is meant by this dry arid wood, this light hay, this stubble, which is the plaything of the wind? It is a life of hazard and caprice, of indolence and uselessness, of egoism and sensuality; it is life in the intoxication and giddiness of the things here below. Do you know what is meant by gold, silver, diamonds, and pearls? It is a life regulated, made useful, mortified, and united to God. These are the majestic stories which will rise on the foundation and complete the edifice, if you will allow them.

To-day we shall speak of the regulated life.

I.

WHAT IS THE REGULATED LIFE?

You must distinguish well between the life of *rule,* the *regular life,* and the *regulated life.*

[1] I Cor., xiv, 34.

The life of rule is that which submits all the movements, actions, and, in consequence, all the will, to a positive rule: it is the life of religious communities; this perfection would not be in keeping with the life of the world.

The regular life is that which conforms in general to the commandments of God and the Church. It is said of a man who keeps Sunday, makes his Easter, and whom we suppose by that to be faithful to his other duties, that he is *regular*.

But between the life of rule for the least actions, and the regular life for the principal christian acts, the regulated life is found—the life that follows certain rules, and does not abandon the ordinary actions, and the employment of time, to the unforeseen or caprice. Under this head, we say of a person that her time is well *regulated*.

There is no *regulated life without a regular life*, because it would miss the first and indispensable rule; and we should not call in this sense that life a regulated one which allows study, for instance, to go beyond religious bounds, or that regulates its order by mania or the search for comfort. But a life can be *regular*, without being the least in the world *regulated*, and we see even pious people, who live without order, without rule, without exactness; in a most deplorable disorder.

The *regular* life has many degrees, from strict and languishing duty, to fervent piety and devotion, which is the flame of charity. The *regulated* life has its degrees also, from the observance of some very generous points, to a life of rule, such as it can be practised in the world.

The *regular* life attaches itself to duties through negligence and dissipation; the *regulated* life attaches itself to actions through indolence and frivolity.

II.

Principle of the Regulated Life.

1st. To have a rule for the principal actions.

To get up and *go to bed* at a time *in proportion* to your waking hours, but not to put sleep off indefinitely by some frivolous reading; not to prolong night into day by sloth and indolence, or by the vanity of good form. By changing everything, we reach the point of persuading ourselves that by rising late we give ourselves quite a fashionable air and tone; so much so, that now young people would think they had lost their elegance, perhaps even their nobility, if they could not say, with a very amiable abandon: "I get up sometime about noon."

We insist on this point of rising, and, in consequence of the bed hour, because it is the regulating point of the day; for on it depends the meditation, the habit of hearing Mass, time for everything, even the interior order of the household.

2nd. *Meditation.*—I do not think there is a person, with good will, who could not give twenty minutes, including the vocal prayers, to a prepared meditation. But this must be done the first thing, so that you will not be encroached upon by anything that may turn up—unless you can be sure of being able to give the time to it at church, before Mass.

Mass.—This is an ancient and pious custom which was formerly practised, I will not say by fervent persons, but by all who were not obliged to go to manual labour at early dawn. A doctor assisted at Mass before going on his sick calls, a magistrate before going to court; and when Fenelon draws his portrait of the indolent man whose life is utterly useless, we are astonished to find that this good-for-nothing assisted at Mass each day in a good-for-nothing way. The workman and the labourer even, in pious districts, found time to fill this devotion, and had the pious habit of attending a very early Mass, as well as servants.

At all events, the daily assistance at Mass should be at a fixed hour, in order to regulate the service of others, and punctuality in the house by it. This hour, according to general rule, should not be a *late one*. Ordinarily, I should say the earliest at seven o'clock, and the latest at nine.

If this habit of daily Mass has great drawbacks, you should at least practise it at certain times, such as Lent, Advent, Ember days, and days of devotion; not only those that are kept by popular customs, such as certain feasts of the Blessed Virgin, but those that are kept through piety, such as the feast of the Holy Angels, and many others.

A quarter of an hour of *spiritual* reading, two decades of the *rosary*, and three on Saturdays, said at the most convenient time, or in church in connection with *a visit to the Blessed Sacrament*, will sustain you admirably through the naggings and sometimes *exhaustions* of the day, which should end with an *examination of conscience*, where the active and passive must be quietly gone over—that is, the good you have done, the victories won, the wrong committed, and the negligence that has predominated in your life.

These are the principal spiritual exercises.

Regulate, in as far as it is possible, the ordinary and common actions, such as receptions, visits, outings, shopping, correspondence, recreation, work, household details, good works outside. I say in as far as it is possible, because nothing can be altogether regulated on these points, because calm and amiable piety should preserve a smoothness of life, and never go to the extent of mania, narrowness, and ridicule, for if one is the servant and child of God, these two qualities should produce a noble liberty, which neither the slave nor the machine can have.

3d. Not to fail through negligence or caprice to do what you have laid out for yourself, the object of the regulated life being to overcome our natural inconstancy and the immortification of the will.

But, on the other hand, no obstinacy or narrowness of spirit; make the rule give way before necessity, duty, charity, politeness even. St. Louis of Gonzaga, in receiving an inopportune visit, which deprived him of hearing a sermon, consoled himself gaily and said: "I should go to the sermon in order to learn how to overcome self; here I can practise that empire over self at once."

St. Francis of Sales, who led a life of rule, having one day said Mass later than usual in a chateau, would not make his thanksgiving, in order not to keep the dinner waiting which had been announced. This is the order and the liberty of the children of God.

III.

ADVANTAGES OF THE REGULATED LIFE.

There are some very good persons, and pious to a certain point, who have an irritating antipathy, a creeping aversion for this regulated life, the bare *idea* of which (because they do not expose themselves to it) unhinges and overwhelms them.

Material and domestic disorder is the element which goes with their conduct; the life of loafing, the unexpected, disorder, whim and extreme fantasies, is the water in which they like to struggle on a venture and to their fancy; a life of order for such persons, is what air would be to the fish.

They may be more or less guilty before God—I shall not examine that point; but this disposition is always unpleasant and disheartening to those around us, injurious to business, ruinous to duties, and sometimes causes deplorable consequences.

With the regulated life on the contrary:

1st. There is time for everything, and what the spirit of order can accomplish in the way of duties, useful things, and joys, even in a day, is incredible. The days have only twenty-four hours, but one would say they had forty-eight; while disorderly persons do nothing, accomplish nothing, have time for nothing; they say there is nothing so hurried as a person who has nothing to do.

I know that this inconvenience makes but slight impression on indolent hearts, but when we come to speak of the useful life, they will have to examine whether God, society, the nobility alone of life, could accommodate itself to such a sterile existence; besides, the want of order weighs on them, at least as a preventative to a larger share of enjoyment, and the calm necessary to flavour it.

2nd. With the regulated life, there is a holy use of time, a great conformity to the will of God, who has put order everywhere, and who wishes it in the smallest details of His works. The employment of our moments, of which we should be very careful, is the small change of the sum exacted to gain heaven; there is no time that flows, that will not be of use for eternity.

3d. There is a great calm communicated to the soul, and with this calm a rare dignity of conduct; the calm of life always implies great superiority. Have you ever happened to have approached one of those men of God, whose life, being under the subjection of a rule, seemed to run so smoothly, with such liberty of mind and heart? You were stupified by the calm with which he heard you, as if your affair were the only one in the world; little by little your agitation ceases—you enter into a peaceful atmosphere, and leave thoroughly impressed with this peace. The secret of these men is their life of order, and without penetrating into that sanctuary, which nothing troubles, every time you approach a superior man of this class, either to expose the infirmities of the body, to confide the difficulties of your affairs, or to treat of the interests which pertain to the administration, you will be astonished at the calm which listens, at the calm which answers. It is because the superior soul is exalted enough to maintain itself in the tranquility of order; the agitation of the winds does not reach the summit of high mountains, and storms are formed from the vapours of the earth.

4th. With the life of order there is *punctuality*. Punctuality! it has been called the politeness of kings; I should prefer to call it the politeness of virtue, the politeness of woman.

You receive many reproaches on this subject, Ladies, and while I know for a certainty that the other half of the human kind is not always innocent, it is with you that I am concerned. Punctuality, this polish of all virtues, this sweet varnish of all qualities, I cannot recommend too strongly to you; this condition without which, they will not give you credit for a thousand other virtues.

Tardiness comes from a lack of order, from vanity, and immortification. Tardiness is a lack of charity towards those who are kept waiting, and does great wrong to oneself, for they count the faults of those for whom they wait. Nothing weakens the esteem and affection of a husband to a greater extent; and, if I may speak humanly, the exterior charm, on which a woman places so much importance, is destroyed by the irritation and agitation which the constant lack of punctuality causes. Do not content yourself with a beauty which remains, notwithstanding, and which is to be paraded in a circle that has not been kept waiting, or at least has waited with more indifference; this triumph, which you exaggerate, is very futile, and not as assured as you think; it is worth but little, while your tardiness has made great losses where it should have made great gain; for beauty, remember it well, Ladies, is not only the reflection of the soul on the features, it is above all, the refraction of this reflection, in the soul of those who contemplate it, and when seen through tardiness, which displaces it, the eye reflects only the faults.

5th. Finally, with the regulated life we acquire gently the habit of overcoming self, and by the efforts of each instant we acquire the life of mortification, of which I shall speak particularly.

It is great wisdom:

To *do* what we *should* do.

To *do well* what we do.

To do *each thing* in its time.

One day on entering a school I stood in admiration before this inscription:

A place for everything;

And everything in its place.

Ladies, apply these axioms to your conduct.

But let us go a little higher.

Peace is the tranquility of order; the work of the day should be done in its day. Jesus Christ could say: "I always do the things that please the Father."[1] I say to you, as the desire of the happiest, may the God of peace give you aptitude for all kinds of good, so that, in doing His will, you may accomplish in you that which is pleasing in His eyes.

---

[1] John, VIII, 29.

WOMAN'S SUNDAY.

Opus diei, in die suo.
"Let the work of the day be done in its day."

THERE is a portion of our life which God has set apart for His special service. It is a tenth or rather a seventh of our existence, which He takes from our entire liberty; a seventh of the week, a seventh of the year, and in consequence a seventh of our life, figured by Sunday in His periodical cycle; this portion the Lord has reserved for Himself by a solemn consecration.

So if life itself should be regulated, how much more reason have we for submitting to rule this portion of our life which does not belong to us, and the use of which the Lord has the rigorous right to determine! If the work of the day should be done in its day, *opus diei, in die suo;* with what accuracy should the work of God be done in God's day!

This follows our last instruction very naturally; that is why I speak to you to-day of the *Sanctification of Sunday by women*.

This sacred and essential principle, that Sunday is a day apart, a day reserved, a day that God has taken of our existence, and in consequence that God has the right to regulate is what must be laid down the first thing. So He has ordered that this day shall be consecrated to Him, that it shall be *His* day, not only a day when we must do something for Him, but a day which belongs to Him, and which we must consecrate to His service. Sunday, then, is God's day, *His day*, because it belongs to Him; *His day*, because it is the one on which He receives in a special manner our visits and our homage. This is the mother and life-giving idea of the sanctification and observance of this day.

So the holiness of Sunday consists in two things:

1st. The cessation of servile work or manual labour.

2nd. The sanctification of the day by religious exercises.

I.

Women on their part should neither work on this day nor cause others to work at forbidden things.

1st. *Not to work.*

Owing to their habitually recluse and sedentary life, women do not know what to do with themselves on Sunday; they are without ease—I was going to say without grace—if they have not a piece of work in their hands.

From this comes the *illusion* of what is forbidden in work on Sunday.

Torture to occupy the fingers without violating the prohibition.

In general, needle work of all kinds, sewing, embroidery, and knitting, *are forbidden.*

But immediately an excuse is brought forth against the prohibition; the activity of the tongue, rather than that of the fingers, is employed in drawing-rooms. Every Sunday, and even during the week, drawing-rooms are turned into universities, where handiwork is warmly discussed, always to prove that it is permitted. "It is not to make money:" wrong reason;—"it is for the poor, for the Church:" wrong reason;—"it is better to work than to gossip:" it has been discovered that this remedy for gossipping is not efficacious. "One does not know what to do with oneself, one is bored to death;"—and then when they are at their wit's end they pile up the attacks pell-mell: "we have permission," "it is ridiculous, impossible; alone we can make out, can settle ourselves; but when we have guests, what is to become of us?"

In all this I only see one real reason; that is, that you are bored, and you add: "to death," from the habit of exaggeration. But this *ennui*, is precisely the sacrifice of *dependence* which God asks of *your liberty*.

What! the simple labourer for whom it is necessary every day to gain his bread, he must give God this servitude, and you rich whom God has loaded with liberty, will you pay Him this small homage so unwillingly!

What! your servants are bored by waiting in an ante-chamber or on the seat of a carriage; your *maids* are bored to death, and to sleep, by waiting for you into the middle of the night; and you servants of God, you cannot carry a few hours of inaction, once a week! They are paid for that, you will say, it is their duty and their condition. Do not speak thus, your heart would disown such hard words. Besides, do you imagine that you are in the service of God gratuitously? Are not your wages high enough for you to fill some duties for the Sovereign Master, who has loaded you with gifts?

What! you have six days of rest, of pleasure, of liberty, of fancy work for the Church, the poor, trifles of furniture, and the frivolities of dress; and you do not think it enough! that it is too much to show your dependence on God by *one day out of seven*, when the rest of your kind are subject *six days* to the dependence of work, and still should consecrate *the seventh* to God!

Ah! let us leave, let us leave this inferior region of the drawing-room; it is badly chosen ground for the discussion of a stitch or a crochet, a flower, or a bit of tapestry; the needles would stick, and the tongues would disconcert still more, the poor theologian working in this hive, where everyone is buzzing.

Let us ascend to a sufficiently high region not to be able to hear these little fretful, fretting cries; and there, soaring in the atmosphere of God, we shall judge sanely what is permitted, and what not. Let us ascend to the throne of God (it is very far from your drawing-rooms and your work tables), and there see the Sovereign Master of life regulating the days of man and weighing them in His divine hands. Out of seven, He leaves six of them free; the *seventh* He reserves for Himself; *He blesses it*, separates it from profane use and work; *He sanctifies it*, consecrates it to His service.

You will never be able to change this eternal law; and if you disturb the divisions of these days and their employment, there is *disorder*.

The seventh day, or Sunday, is then God's, it is His day, and not yours; you cannot dispose of it as you wish, and God can prescribe what He pleases for it.

The six days of the week are abandoned to your work or your leisure, as you please; but *one day out of seven* God demands the *sacrifice of your liberty*.

Is it asking too much, Ladies? I appeal to your justice, to your compassion for your brethren, to your gratitude towards God, to your religious tact, your feminine delicacy.

While respecting the prohibition of manual labour, you set your wits to work to know how to occupy your fingers. And here there is truly genius, each one has invented her little work for Sunday.

You wind, you roll, you unroll. You cut, you prepare, you paint, you roll paper into spirals and fringe them into bunches. It is as simple as the folding of a paper into the form of a boat or a bird; and you vaunt these proceedings as occupying your fingers without violating the *Sunday rest.*

Let me tell you at once that none of this *is forbidden*, understand well, *it is not forbidden.*

But mercy! what a rage to always have something in your hands on Sunday! not to wish to make it different from other days! not to wish to submit to the suspension of your liberty!

At least, let your sitting-rooms have a *Sunday air*, do not have your tables crowded as on other days of the week; for it is an air which hurts that delicacy born of fidelity.

But it can be said with certainty, that if the Church had prescribed a little work suitable for

Sunday, if it *exacted* of you, for instance, a hundred rolled lamp-lighters, you would engineer how to do without this command, you would never find time to do it, and reasons would not be wanting to find it ridiculous.

But we must always return to this point, that Sunday is a day of dependence, that it belongs to God, that God has wished to make us feel, *even by a little ennui*, that the day is not ours, and that we must acknowledge our servitude.

For the man of manual and habitual labour, Sunday is a day of *liberty*, which God imposes on him that he may be able to apply himself to his religion and to rest. For the man who does not live by the work of his hands, the obliged rest places him under the hand of God in a dependence all the more obligatory, since he is not bound to work for six days, consequently should show himself all the more grateful.

The working man has only a few hours for himself, then Sunday; and you women of leisure and enjoyment have but a few hours in one day out of seven to overcome yourselves, will you refuse to God this small tribute?

The working man, bent under the weight of duty all the week, feels terribly his dependence on God. But you, by the sacrifice of a few hours only, have more need *than he* to feel your dependence on God, and to prove it.

However, see how light the Church, in the name of God, has made this proof! it only forbids you needle work, other things you can do. But, is it *delicate* to engineer in one way, and another to escape this servitude? Is it *delicate* to see your sitting-rooms only respect the letter of the law and not the spirit; without wrong (I repeat it) but also without the wish to break your will, or to bend under the hand of God? Is it *delicate* not to submit to a little material ennui when you can vary it with a walk, visits, conversation, reading, music, and drawing?

Ah! judge what is done and said from this side of the consideration, it will be the best refutation of all your pretexts.

2nd. *Not to make others work.*

This concerns men more particularly; they have a great responsibility on this point. But women have their part also of honourable fidelity to it, both indoors and out of doors.

1st. To watch over the servants' *respect* for Sunday; but in recompense to leave them some time *for themselves* during the week.

2nd. To see to things *beforehand*, so as not to require any mending or fixing of your clothes of any consequence; of course, a few urgent or unforeseen stitches are not forbidden.

3rd. Not to give an order on *Saturday evening* and demand it on *Monday morning*, even though you tell the seamstress not to work *for you* on Sunday. You see that the warning is absurd, and the "*for you*" indelicate. You seem to say, work for others as much as you please. . . . .

4th. To have the delicacy to give the dressmaker *sufficient time*, so that she may not be obliged to work on Sunday. And those seamstresses who crowd their delivery till Saturday, and are obliged in consequence often to work all Saturday night into Sunday, would do much better to distribute their work wisely during the week, and if necessary to work all Friday night, rather than Saturday, so as not to be worn out by their watch on Sunday. There are *some exceptions of urgency* here; these exceptions prove the rule, and belong to individual direction.

5th. *To foresee purchases*, and never to buy anything on Sunday but through necessity. The best means of closing shops is not to buy. Those who find this a difficult rule, should visit protestant countries, and they would be embarrassed . . . . *Transite ad insulas Cethim.* . . . .

3rd. What can then be done on Sunday?

1st. No forbidden work—if necessary, be willing to be a little bored; it is a day of service and dependence, which does not belong to us, and of which we are not masters. Put this great principle in the mind, and a little of the love of God in the heart, and you will not be bored, or you will bear a little *ennui* bravely.

2nd. Reading, correspondence (I am not speaking here of religious exercises), music, drawing, walks, visits of pleasure or charity, social reunions, the usual charm of which is destroyed on one side by the *smoke* which the men exhale, and on the other by the *needle*, which deaden the animation of intercourse and the commerce of life.

3rd. Finally, give a part of the day to religious works.

II.

The cessation of work on Sunday is one of the great purposes of the day.

For the working man, *rest* is the *means* given him to apply himself to the things of God, and heaven. For the man who is free and independent by his fortune, it is *the call* to his great religious duty.

When the wealthy class do not bend under their duty to God, while the workman is obliged to bend continually under the things of earth, it engenders a discontent in society to the extent of exciting irritation, this irritation ferments but little in peace and order, but bursts forth on the day of trouble and combat.

On this day, then, which belongs to the Lord, we belong so little to ourselves, that we cannot do *what we wish*, and are obliged to do *that which perhaps we do not care to do*. My feet wish to be quiet, but they must carry me to the house of God.

This sublime idea, which makes us recognize a master, this homage, all the more eligible in a position which is free, exalted, and loaded with benefits, is the soul and life of the precepts, and in particular of the sanctification of holy days, abstinences, and alms; and greatly increases fidelity to religious observances.

If you have *this life* in the heart,

I shall only tell you that assisting at Mass on Sunday is of *rigorous precept*. Beyond hearing this Mass, the Church has prescribed nothing, she confines herself to exhortations.

But I do not know that it is forbidden to *exhort* the faithful to religious works on holy days, or that one would be more to blame in *exhorting* them to that, than in exhorting them to the exercises of the month of May, retreats, perpetual adorations, and other pious acts.

I shall *exhort* you, then (notice: it is an exhortation):

1st.[1] Not to frequent *late low masses* by custom or tone, only to go through necessity or obstacle. Formerly the altar, at which these masses were said, in the Cathedral of Paris, was called *altare pigrorum;* to-day it is too often the altar for laziness,

[1] This applies to Catholic countries only, where sometimes low mass is said at noon.

dress, worldliness; the habituées of the noon low mass have not a great reputation for fervour.

2nd. To go to the parochial and the High Mass. If on the one hand, it is not of precept, on the other it is true that a christianity can scarcely be conceived of, where the word of God is never heard, where the advice of the Church is never received, where all the worship consists in a cold and unintelligent assistance at the August Sacrifice.

3rd. To go when there is nothing to prevent you to Vespers: not to confine yourself constantly to Benediction as though you were flying from the word of God.

4th. To seek in these public exercises the general and common edification, avoiding *exclusiveness* and all those little *sequestrations* where self-love is nourished, but which do not give rise to good example and general animation.

5th. On this day to do some spiritual reading, good works, visiting the poor and the sick, and to choose, as far as possible, Sunday and holy days for the reception of the Sacraments.

6th. To break with the world where it ruins or weakens the sanctification of God's day: such as

Saturday evening receptions, which destroy the holy morning by fatigue; *Sunday evening receptions* which absorb the day by preparations and often purchases; *Sunday afternoons* which expose you to visitors at the hour of religious services.

7th. To watch well over those who depend on you that they *can* and *do* hear Mass; to give them also both the *time* for, and the *example* of so doing.

8th. To arrange to the best of your ability, according to the conditions and difficulties of the household, that Sunday may not seem like other days, and may be really sanctified.

9th. Finally that Sunday should reanimate, vivify, and give life to the week which it begins, is also a great object of the day.

Man is not only obliged to *observe* Sunday, he is constituted the *guardian* of it: *Custodite sabbata mea*. Sunday you shall *keep;* let us take this word in its most beautiful acceptation.

But woman above all has become the *guardian* of the honour and sanctity of this day; it is a *guard of honour* which God bestows on her with its orders and commands. 1st, Because the greater part of the work which must be suspended, and the purchases which must be avoided, come from the woman and her pious supervision. 2d, Because it is reserved for her attention to remove the difficulties which might arise, to watch over the fidelity of the children and the servants. 3d, Because the rest of God should be called *delicate*, and treated with delicacy; and the delicacy of fidelity, is the appendage of woman. 4th, Because, finally, the example of sanctification should come *above all*, from her regular conduct, and her influence as wife, mother, and mistress of the house.

THE USEFUL LIFE.

Succidite arborem ut quid etiam terram occupat?
"Cut it down therefore, why cumbereth it the ground? Luke, XIII, 7.

LIFE will never be *useful* unless it is *regulated;* but a regulated life is not always a useful one.

I know of regulated lives where time is seriously used to plunge oneself into idle studies, researches which flatter vanity, and collections which unite great trifles.

I know of regulated lives of which the principle of order is an egoism, which does not wish to disturb itself for anything, an indolence which wishes to enjoy its ease, a sensuality which seeks the largest share of enjoyment, a system of well-being which lives by régime and eats at regular hours.

All this is wretched and should make you feel how necessary it is that a *useful life* should be superposed on the foundation of a regulated life; how many lives, that apparently run in order, are exposed to hear that terrible oracle of the Lord:

"*Cut it down therefore, why cumbereth it the ground?*"

Besides the regulated life only consecrates a portion of our moments, and our best moments; but it is question here of utilizing the whole, of spreading over the whole of life the grace of a holy, beneficial utility.

I.

By a useful life, you must not understand *excess*, the indefinite multiplication of religious works. Multiplying them at the expense of other equally as important duties would often cause *disorder*, and always cause *indigestion;* for it is not what we eat that nourishes us, but what we digest, and nourishment has not attained its end until there is assimilation of the food with our substance. Thus St. Bernard adds to these words, "If any one loves me he will keep my word." "Keep the word of God even more carefully than you keep the nourishment of the body; let it pass, so to speak, into the intestines of your soul, let it pass into your affections and your habits."

By the useful life you must not understand that *breathless activity* which strives to invent for itself works of charity, which encumbers itself without order or limit in what is called good works. There is disorder, imprudence, fatigue, breathlessness for oneself and suffocation for others, prevention of the best good, and sometimes deplorable omission of personal duties in this febrile agitation, which has an attraction for woman's nature; and in all cases there is the illusion of imagining that life is only utilized by charitable works; it is the means of neglecting through principle the important duties of the household, the family and society. Here is a case where this word of the Saviour may be applied: "Duties, *you must do; good works, you must not omit.*"

By the *useful* life is meant to fill up the gaps of our day usefully, to give value to our ordinary duties and common actions, and to mingle the element of service to our neighbour with our life. It is in this sense that St. Augustine calls work a prayer; it was the state of the soul of St. Louis of

Gonzaga, to whom it was indifferent whether he died at recreation or not, because he was then in the order of God.

So to make life useful, it is necessary:

1st. To throw aside those false and anti-christian ideas on the subject;

2nd. To put into practice certain vivifying principles.

II.

1st. It is a false and anti-christian idea to imagine that life is given us only to enjoy, to procure the largest share possible of enjoyment for ourselves, that mortification and penance should begin only where it is impossible to find such or such a comfort; finally to esteem life by enjoyment, and to hear christian lips proclaim, that the pagans or certain materialized peoples, *understood* or *understand* life perfectly.

2nd. It is a false and anti-christian idea to think that *all men*, without exception, each in his own sphere of action, are not obliged to work and to make there lives useful in a certain way, or to think that life is sufficiently praiseworthy and utilized when you deign to consent to *occupy yourselves with self*, your fortune, your goods, the increase of your income, or the value of your lands, *being useful only to self*, and not seeking to serve others in proportion to your power and influence.

3rd. It is a false and anti-christian idea to admit that the worthless lives of men and women of fortune are not reproved by God, that they violate no precept, do no wrong, as if the Gospel does not give us very decidedly the idea of crime in a worthless life, when it represents the Lord cursing the *sterile* tree, reproving the *buried* talent, condemning the *worthless* servant.

To have a just and christian idea, we must acknowledge to ourselves: That the useless life,

1st. Is in formal opposition to this general oracle, to this common sentence pronounced against all: "You shall eat your bread by the sweat of your brow." When the sage praised the valiant woman, the woman who had a noble husband, exalted children, extensive estates, numerous servants, and lived in opulence; he declared that, notwithstanding all this nobility, all this fortune, all this ease of life: "She did not eat her bread in idleness."

All brows must be covered with sweat; the sweat of study, of intellectual activity, of public service, is much more exhausting and more difficult to restore than that of work of the body; it must count for something in the general debt.

2nd. The worthless life is injurious to God, who has given *so much*, and who does not give in order to nourish pride and laziness, but shall demand of us in proportion to his gifts; again it is fatal to society where it stirs up envy, irritation, unjust and often odious prejudices. Labourers are not only the workmen of the spade and the hammer; every useful man is a labourer, a workman of God, who accomplishes his work, who fills the duties of his position in the circle of utility traced for him by Providence. The world cannot be divided into producers and consumers, for though consummation is to a certain extent a public utility, it is not positive and personal enough, so that each in his way should *produce*.

3rd. The worthless life is degrading to nobility, which is the soûl of the people, and to wealth which is their heart; there are no natures so strong that they may not be *degenerated* and corrupted by idleness. The useless life, a life which exhales itself only in smoke and the care of certain racing animals, which consumes itself in the reading of novels, or the frivolities of dress, is a life which has already impoverished the strength of a weaker, consequently of a less noble, generation. No, no one's life should be one of amusement, dissipation, frivolous games, useless agitations, insignificant pass-times; the greater part of it should be devoted to serious and useful occupations in conformity to our state.

Let us seize it well: A christian can only be great, noble, rich, freed from a part of the servitude which weighs so heavily on the greater number of the children of Adam, under four conditions:

1st. By detaching his heart from the perishable goods which surround him, without that he is only an egotistical, small, narrow and mean man.

2nd. By persuading himself that he is born to work, in one way or another, and to apply this principle.

3rd. By compensating for all his material advantages, by more humility and devotion.

4th. Beyond this devotion, by giving the most he reasonably can, to his less privileged brothers.

III.

PRINCIPLES OF THE USEFUL LIFE.

1st. To do something, not to be *idle*. Really, women are increditable; on Sunday they put their wits to work (and that is not saying a little) to employ their fingers; and in every day life, they push the wave of indolence and *far niente* to unknown limits.

2nd. Not to be occupied *with nothings*. The genius of being very much occupied in doing nothing, of finding oneself overburdened in the midst of the greatest trifles, is a disheartening secret which certain women possess (and I know a number of men who are women on this point), and cultivate with incredible success.

3rd. To fill first of all and as essential, your duties as wife, mother and mistress of the house. If a widow, says St. Paul, has children, let her learn above all to regulate and govern her household well; and when these widows, reaching the canonical age, wished to consecrate themselves to the Lord, St. Paul exacted that they should give a good account of how they had brought up their family; so sacred are the duties of state of life, that they should never be neglected by the untimely activity of even the most worthy works.

4th. To do each thing in its time and in its place, for fear of mixing up everything and having time for nothing, of fatiguing others and being useless to oneself.

5th. To offer yourselves gently, prudently and with system to be useful in every way to your neighbour, in conversation, where a word well placed can do much, in visits, the price of which is raised when made with charity and amenity, in letters where sincere kindness can edify greatly; now defending the attacked, giving protection to the unprotected, now pouring out help or not refusing counsel, now giving encouragement or spreading consolation, and in all this forgetting self, supporting weariness, braving the repugnances of nature.

6th. To look upon the *works of charity* in which you take part as *an element* of the useful life, but not as constituting it exclusively. Without that all charitable utility will exhaust itself in some meetings, some details of administration, and will leave you no strength for the thousand useful cares of which we have spoken.

7th. To wish seriously to have done something good, something useful for others each day. If a pagan writes at the end of his day when he has not had the opportunity of being useful or helpful: "I have lost my day," what shall we say of christian men and women who have so many days marked with this afflicting note, and who neither care nor regret it! If with this good determination we have succeeded in doing something useful, we shall have a sweet *repose* in the accomplished duty; if, on the contrary, the occasion has not presented itself, the good will held in readiness, will be of great value before God.

St. Paul has thus drawn the progressive order and ordinance of the useful life.

"Whatsoever things are just," this for the essential duties.[1]

"Whatsoever true," this for the real duties.

"Whatsoever holy," this for duties sanctified and exalted by supernatural views and principles.

[1] Phil., IV, 8.

"Whatsoever of good fame," this for the perfume which the useful life diffuses.

"Whatsoever lovely," this for the manner of doing, charming manner, which makes virtue sweet, example attractive. This loveliness, when it is christian, is the small change of charity.

Have, says the Apostle, these just and true views, this worthy and amiable conduct; add to it all that is virtue, discipline, and the God of peace will be with you, He will put the best order in your heart, the most desirable utility in your life.

WOMAN'S CONVERSATION.

> *Os suum aperuit sapientiae, et lex clementiae in lingua ejus.*
> "She hath opened her mouth to wisdom and the law of clemency is on her tongue" Prov., XXXI, 26.

THIS is one of the praises which the Holy Ghost gives to the valiant woman. Let it be said without offense that this noble attribute of man (we alone being responsible for the existence of its sorrows, its maternal care never failing) is the great and nearly the only instructress of man, the edification of our religious assemblies, the apostle of the family, the perfume of charity in the world, the delicate hand which heals our wounds and the sweetest remembrance of a child's heart to the end of his career; again let it be said without offense, that conversation constitutes the greater part of a woman's life, it is the resource of her sedentary life, and far from injuring her various works, it mingles itself with them and animates them.

Thus does religion respect woman, without concealing a *fault*, or rather *an excess* with which she can justly be reproached.

Do you wish to know, now, how *your* world treats you, in what a loose style it allows itself to speak of you? It has dared to formulate, to write this definition: "Woman is a creature that dresses, undresses and gabbles," and it fancies itself very witty.

So important is it, that if there is one thing for woman to *utilize* in a useful life, it is conversation.

It is *necessary* to make your conversation useful, in order that the greater part of your life may not be lost.

There is great good to be done by conversation; it is that sweet and unperceived preaching which becomes the modesty of woman.

We shall examine three things: the conversation of women among themselves, their conversation with men, and the general rules for conversation.

I.

THE CONVERSATION OF WOMEN AMONG THEMSELVES.

I find the first thing two faults in it:

1st. First, its *license*. This word frightens you, and seems, before any examination, slanderous or exaggerated; listen.

It would be wrong to think that women, so admirable in their habitual reserve, so gracious by that perfume of modesty which they spread in public, always keep a pure and embalmed reserve among themselves. One would say, if one were permitted to hear them, that they made up for an official restraint, for an annoyance which was difficult to carry; and after having been beyond the limit of *prudery* and sometimes to the borders of *ridicule* outside, they considered all conversation permitted, once they were no longer on the scene of public life.

Listen to them among themselves; they speak of *an intimacy* which should always have its religious mystery. They expose secrets over which God has thrown the most venerable veils. They question and consult, and as it is called, enlighten each other on rules of morality which should scarcely have their twilight elucidation, and their timid solution elsewhere than in the venerable shade of the sanctuary.

Hence, so many false rules are laid down—so many anti-christian *customs* contracted. They do not blush to discuss the lawful and the unlawful, to deform imprescriptible laws by sanction and forgiveness, and to reduce to the limitations of self-love and vanity that which the heart, purified by religion, alone should decide.

Singular contrast! Above all if they wish to receive or ask advice, when it comes from God in the most venerable secret and under the most sacred veil, they will go in bold face to ask this counsel with frightening details of a light, awkward and often indiscreet person who will abuse it!

I ask your pardon, Ladies, for what I am about to say (and here I ask the experience of mothers); there is a principle and axiom of conduct which still remains, which is, that there is nothing more dangerous for a young woman than familiar society and conversation with persons of her own sex.

2nd. The second fault of the conversation of women among themselves, is the exaggeration of their dignity, their power, their empire and dominion.

In intimacy women make up amply for the pretended yoke which weighs on them in conjugal society. They do not wish to understand that this term *conjugal* indicates that man and woman carry one and the same yoke together in this society; and if it is organized according to the thoughts of God, the man commands with love, the woman obeys with love; the man lowers his authority by loving, the woman lifts her submission to the dignity of loving, and thus each doing his or her part, they establish this level of the common yoke of the most sacred duties. Women do not wish to understand (or men either) that marriage is not the union of two egoisms, but a mutual devotion and attachment. Thus they depict themselves in the intimacy of persons of their own sex; they revolt when they are alone, and far from home they form the most beautiful plans of resistance and dominion. Then they make me think of those rebellious school-children who organize a resistance in form while the master is absent; and when he appears they submit to everything, especially those who have spoken the loudest. We must return these women who understand their true position, and their true dignity so little from a christian standpoint, to the fables : to show them that we have seen many such councils which took this stand for nothing, that when it was question of deliberating the councillors made a great noise; but, when it was question of executing no one was present.

All the same, these private deliberations do the most serious harm. There you form a false idea of your rank and your power, because you take as *acquired* rights and homages a respect and condescension which are only *concessions* made by society, civilized by religion. Lacking power and rights you exaggerate an empire (and you know which one, Ladies), and think you can do every thing; that if one does not reign by right of birth, one can at least govern by right of conquest; that woman possesses in herself an irresistible strength, and that if this strength is unappreciated by coarse beings, she can still vanquish by haughtiness of manner and unbending character, that is, by the most pitiable and saddest of all means.

With these ideas, all woman's counsel stops at this conclusion, which is taken in the most triumphant unanimity; "that all is due to woman," without considering that this debt is only a *gracious* concession which should augment her modesty. That woman should command essentially when God has declared that she should essentially obey and remain under the power of man. That her empire is irresistible, that woman must have her way. When she should understand this axiom better, and see in it only a spirit, connection, order and perseverance which God has given to woman, with a delicate insight which is often very wise in the counsel of affairs and which seems from thence to flow from God and His light.

Hence how many homes troubled, desolated and broken up!

Hence this haughty, cutting style which is so unbecoming, when a sweet modesty would assure supremacy much better.

Hence this pride in the midst of polished homages, pride which savours of the parvenue, and which shows at once that the supremacy is not by right of origin. For my part, I have never been differential towards a woman, giving her, for example, the road, without being almost ill-treated by this species of a sovereign, who understands but badly, the modest dignity in her who is honoured.

II.

Women's Conversation with Men.

The first and the greatest fault of women's conversation with men, is that it scarcely exists, has become a myth, *is wanting*, so that we are obliged to judge and condemn it by *contumacy*.

Yes, let us regret that intercourse (*vesari cum*), that which indicates a happy mingling of life, a sort of chain in the polite world, let us regret I say that conversation is no longer what it should be; the *common tribute* of the two parties of the human race, where each one gives his or her side, share, and view.

When both men and women paid this tribute to a purely religious civilization (for remark well that outside of religion the woman is always abandoned, banished, the Arab for example, is satisfied when, with other men, he smokes in silence, breathes aromatic vapours or talks of his horse); in this mingling of life, the woman took instinctively of man's dignity and seriousness; the man, gentleness and delicacy from the woman, to form a society full of strength and charm. It was agreed upon to redouble the respect, even to leave the sceptre to the weaker party, which became the stronger by a holy use of its dignity. But the sceptre in such hands was neither a *rough stick* that struck and wounded, nor a *changeable reed* that bent with every wind. This sceptre was solid, pure, and above all, polite. A just temperament resulted from it which dictated the laws, usages, and even the language to society, and based all on what is true, orderly, just, honest, amiable and delicate.

This happy combination of strength and grace which God has put in the physical order, and which He has inspired for the social order, is tending day by day to be destroyed; and what was most elegant,

French conversation; most exquisite, French politeness; seem to lose themselves in the customs of non-civilized peoples, or in the phlegmatic indifference of peoples who have degenerated from civilization; we are scarcely French any longer, we are becoming Arabs, or we are copying in a servile way customs which do not go with our national character.[1]

Habits, which I do not qualify, a language confined to the stable or politics, has changed everything. Men have formed *circles,* which are no longer concentric; *clubs,* which women cannot frequent; they have called them *casinos, chambers,* that is to say, partitions—they have even dared to give them the name of *society* when they are positively the ruin of it. Then woman abandoned, gave herself up without bounds to her natural frivolity; wounded, she became incensed and tried to revenge herself by haughtiness and a domineering tone which suits her so badly; and then when she could no longer stand her isolation, her only means of approaching the men was to sacrifice reserve

[1] While this paragraph refers particularly to the French, there is much that may be applied to ourselves.

and propriety by tolerating or adopting deplorable tastes.

From that came two faults which have succeeded in corrupting that which the separation had terribly weakened.

1st. *The sporting type.* Woman's mouth is deformed when it opens to speak of smoking, arms, dogs, horses, politics, and noisy hazardous matches. And if by enthusiasm the mouth speaks from the abundance of the heart, and above all, as the result of a distressing habit, there is something disorderly and repugnant in it. Outwardly, men seem to applaud these eccentricities; among themselves they do them justice by ridicule and even contempt. Wait until it is question of choosing a companion for life; they will always want a *woman;* a *sport* would not seem to be of the same nature.

2nd. Second fault: *The blue stocking type* (or of another colour if you wish); it was perhaps a little too severe to say that ink was not suited to certain fingers; there are certain selections of writings which we should regret not to owe to the dictation of woman. But let us say, what is absolutely true, that the shade of the tree of science was mortal for our common mother. With woman, instruction should only dominate on the condition that it develops her heart, and envelops it with a very tight cloak lined with modesty.[1]

Without this there is impropriety, sufficiency, a sharp, arrogant, domineering manner; that is to say, a complete displacement of woman's character. If she experiences resistance in this degradation, she falls still lower, she becomes the *abused woman*, she aspires to the *club* of *rehabilitation*; as if the woman who understands her dignity, and who in her real dignity will always be appreciated, had not been greatly and nobly rehabilitated by the Gospel!

III.

After having pointed out the general defects, let us indicate the positive rules for conversation.

1st. That which must be avoided.

Affectation. You have *two voices*, one for the home; this one is natural, easy, and sometimes has a certain charm about it; the other, for the stage

[1] Some allowance must here be made for the date of these discourses, 1864; high education for women having made rapid strides since then.

of the world, that stage where the greatest danger in the fashionable world is precisely the *comedy* which each one plays on it; for it is after these factitious representations that reputations are established, and engagements for life are concluded! The voice for the world is strained, cutting and often ungracious. A pretentious and studied manner kills the ease of conversation, because it proves that the person who uses it is thinking only of self, of the effect she produces and not in the slightest of *conversing* with others. She arranges her mouth, her voice, and her words as she arranges the folds of a garment according to such or such a shade; then there is no longer any more conversation; common-place remarks are devised, each asks the other about his health, to have a phrase which does not cost anything to say, and *ennui* is the only result for those who question, as for those who answer.

Frivolity. You complain, Ladies, of the fashions; you are the ones who cause their tyranny by being such complacent slaves to them, and by treating their onerous, futile and expensive trifles so seriously!

Add this word of the Gospel to your conversation: "They shall render an account of every idle word,"[1] that is, of every word which is useless to the person who says it, or to the one who hears it, and you will have judged your conversations more severely than I should dare do.

I could never understand those *extremes* that meet in women; a generous, incontestible nobility in feelings, a small distressing frivolity in words. One would say that the mouth did not speak from the abundance of the heart with her.

Rivalry. Do not forget that the *soul* of conversation is to make your own forgotten, in order that that of others, may come out and be of value. This is a science which some worldlings possess the secret of, through interest or vanity; but see what this science is when God lifts it up and inspires it: " Let love be without dissimulation. Loving one another with the charity of brotherhood, with honour preventing one another. Rejoice with them that rejoice, weep with them that weep. If it be possible as much as is in you, having peace with all men."[2]

Finally *slander*. This vice which comes from rivalry, envy; from the uneasiness of the heart at

[1] Matt., XII, 36.   [2] Romans, XII, 9, 10, 15, 18.

the sight of the success of others; less than that, from some lines of the face; less than that again, from a dress, a costume, a jewel; still less than that, often from the inimitable way in which all this is worn.

Slander, an atrocious evil in itself, a terrible evil in its consequences, is produced in the world in three ways, which are always perfidious; by a *heedless way of speaking*, for which one applauds oneself in advance, as for a frankness which has its merit, as for a mouth of gold, which in reality is only a common ditch where reputations are buried, under the pretext of reforming mankind, of telling each one his duty, of calling things by their names, or of constituting oneself the minister of God to avenge his rights. "*I adore slander!*" I have heard this frightful remark. Slander is produced most frequently under the form of *commiseration*. "Poor Madam such a one, how she must suffer! You know? Don't they say?" This pity is only a perfidious evil in disguise. Finally, slander is produced by *pious and discreet reticence*, sometimes by a simple sigh which animates a guilty silence; this is the height of perfidy, for instead of denying and reproving, you let fall a most dubious word which leaves everything to be supposed, and you veil this distressing mirage with a still more distressing compendium; "*Let us pray ! ! !*"

2nd. *What good may be drawn from conversation.*

Woman is surrounded in the world with homage and respect, which she owes to civilization through the Gospel. If she thinks that she exercises a right, or that she rejoices in a conquest, she is mistaken, it is only a concession, a privilege, a favour. Considered as a *right*, her social supremacy would make her haughty, overbearing, without charm, and above all ridiculous; considered as a *concession* and a christian concession, the place accorded to woman makes her still more modest; but in this modesty she finds new grace, a sweet and strong authority, a supremacy which can no longer be disputed, and placed at this modest height which becomes her real rank, the word of woman finds but few censors, rarely contradiction, often subjugates, or at least entices.

For what good cannot a word do that one is obliged to respect, that is supported by modesty and grace, and that draws its authority from the truest charms.

The words and conversation of women can also become a sweet, insinuating, capable and unperceived preaching, and do a thousand times more good than the most renowned sermon.

Woman *reigns* in the world—and—she *governs* also; hence she has all the responsibility of power.

Hence to her, if she understands her modest authority and her mission of reserve, limit, and sweetness, to her;

To soften discussions by one of those words which resemble the gentle rain;

To defend and honour religion;

To establish good and noble customs;

To stigmatize the duel;

To condemn immodest dressing;

To blame eccentricities of pleasure;

To brand overflowing luxury;

And if to the ability of words, to this mysterious strength which weakness possesses, which has produced the saying: " A woman must have her way," she joins above all the perfume of example,—what victories does she not gain for good!

You cannot meditate too much, Ladies, on the words of St. James, in connection with this subject.

"If any man offend not in word, the same is a perfect man: He is also able with a bridle to lead about a whole body."[1]

"Behold how small a fire, what a great wood it kindleth! and the tongue is a fire, a world of iniquity."

"But the tongue no man can tame, an unquiet evil full of deadly poison."

"By it we bless God and the Father, and by it we curse men—"

"Out of the same mouth proceedeth blessing and cursing."

"And if any man think himself to be religious and not bridling his tongue, but deceiving his own heart, that man's religion is vain."[2]

---

[1] James, III, 2, 5, 8, 9, 10.   [2] James, I, 26.

THE LIFE OF UNION WITH GOD.

> *Providebam Dominum in conspectu meo*
> *semper Psalm*
> "I set the Lord always in my sight"
> Psalm, xv, 8

WHO speaks thus, Ladies? Who has revealed this secret to us of a life united to God, of a heart that always walks in the presence of God? Is it the daughter of Phanuel, the old prophetess Ann, who has retired into the temple since her widowhood, never leaving the holy place, serving God there day and night by continual fasting and prayer? Is it one of those contemplative souls who in her footsteps, fled into solitude, from the bustle and contradictions of the world; who obtained the wings of the dove to soar in spirit and heart into the superior regions of the meditation of celestial things? No, Ladies, this word is from a man higher than you in the grandeurs of earth, more occupied than you in affairs and cares here below, more distracted by, and drawn into the things of the world than you; it is the word of a king. It is the word of David who declares that in the midst of the overwhelming affairs of the administration of a kingdom; in the midst of the cares and clamorous anxieties of war; in the midst of the surroundings, seductions and pleasures without end, he had always the thought of God before him, and that his life was constantly vivified by the presence of God: *Providebam Dominum in conspectu meo semper.*

So, it is this model of a *life in union with God* which I have proposed to you to-day.

The *regulated* life consecrates certain actions. The *useful* life fructifies the whole of our moments. The *life of union with God* completes this plentitude of the spiritual life, and becomes the great resource of the life of rule, of the life of christian utility. It is as it were an atmosphere, in which we have in a free, and consequently in a meritorious way, our being, our movement, and our life.

Let us define quietly this life of union with God, so as to leave nothing vague in the imagination or in practice: It consists in the happy habit of the *presence of God*, in the calm and easy practice of *raising* our heart frequently to the things of heaven.

I.

This life of union with God, such as I have defined it, is not a mystic invention, an exaltation which has fermented in convents.

But, first of all, let us renounce this error of always putting the *idea of the cloister*, that is to say, of the religious and most perfect life, in the distance, as something heterogeneous, which has no participation in the christian life. The religious state, *in its spirit*, is nothing more than the development, the perfection of christianity; it is not estranged from it, it deals with the whole of it. Certain forms, certain *exterior* practices peculiar to the religious life, are purely *accidental to it.* The cloister is not an island entirely separated from the *continent of the Gospel*, it is a peninsula which holds to the continent of christianity by the large base of its baptismal engagements, then extricates itself and advances into the ocean of the perfection of the counsels.

Nothing, on the contrary, is more *elementary*, more *classic*, if I dare to express myself thus, than the life of union with God. It has been frequently practised in lives in the world, in great, broad and very busy lives.

For the ancient just man, the Holy Ghost has consecrated this expression: "He walked with the Lord." And the Lord said to Abraham: "I am the Almighty God; walk before me and be perfect."[1] St. Paul made his normal respiration of this life: "The Lord," he said, "in whose presence I walk." Thus I do not know that these great personages, so closely united to God, were ever counted among the disciples of St. Benedict or St. Francis, among the children of St. Dominic or St. Ignatius.

And notice the word which the Holy Ghost has chosen to portray this life : *walk*, walk in the presence, under the eye; this word *walk* indicates a practice, a habit of something which does not disturb the *walk* of life, which mingles itself on the contrary, with all its steps, and takes up with facility all its movements, all its windings.

Nothing is more natural to the mind and heart of man. See him when he is preoccupied with

[1] Gen., XVII, 1.

the affairs, interests and solicitudes of the world ; when he pursues an end, a passion on earth, he *walks*, he moves in this preoccupation, it absorbs him to the extent of making him seem absent-minded, he speaks of it to himself, and sometimes aloud. But when preoccupation is gentle and regulated, far from fatiguing or encumbering action, it gives wings to thought, energy to the heart, resources to the will, life and perseverance to all the movements. Man watches and sleeps, acts and rests, thinks and speaks with the object which attracts his heart; if there is work, he likes the fatigue of it; if there is slavery, he does not feel the weight of the chains.

II.

Thus, this practice of union with God, should not be reserved for the cloister, secluded in the cloistered life.

It is a practice which is essentially *christian* and *natural*, and is more necessary in the world where everything tends to dissipation, than in the cloister where everything tends to recollection, in the world where everything leads one *from* God, than in the cloister where everything draws one *to* God.

This life of union supposes first of all, the first and fundamental union, the union of our mind with God by a sincere and complete faith; the union of our heart by the state of grace retained, preserved or repaired; the union of our life, augmented by the participation of the Sacraments, and above all by that which is called, par excellence, *Communion*.

But beyond this life essential to the just soul, the life of union which I have just recommended, nourishes the habit of the presence of God, of the simple and easy elevation of the soul towards God—

In our principal actions;

In our difficult duties;

In our temptations;

In our occasions of sin;

In our habitual troubles;

In our acute pains;

In our overwhelming distractions;

In the reunions of the world;

In our depression and *ennui;*

In our bitter impressions;

In the inconsistencies of the will;

In the benefits and consolations of God;

This union consists in a certain tendency, which is the secret and charm of pious souls, to find God in everything, to turn the ordinary life, the most simple occasions, the most indifferent things to God.

To practice this union, it supposes besides the state of grace, that God is *the God of our heart*, that we love Him as He wishes to be loved, perfectly, above all else, that we do not make an acephalous devotion for ourselves, that is to say, that we do not *decapitate* the christian life, by retrenching the sincere practice of the first and greatest of the commandments, from our religious exercises.

III.

Advantages of the Life of Union with God.

1st. It supplies the place of those exercises which we cannot do. We are greedy, Ladies, for these exercises; we are perfectly well aware that there is a great void and coldness in the heart for God; and getting on the wrong path, we wish to fill this void, to chase out this cold, by piling up practices on practices, communions (and why should I not say it?) on communions, without troubling ourselves with the fruit they should produce. "We act for God," says Fenelon, "as we act for the world," where we multiply to give a wrong impression, and above all not to lose our reputation for amiability, and gracious reception, where we multiply, I say, formalities, false attentions, exaggerations of language, in proportion to the *ennui* or annoyance which certain disagreeable and tiresome persons cause us.

In this state, breathless in the pursuit of exercises and practices, we complain incessantly of being disturbed, retained, absorbed; but union with God never disturbs or absorbs one; it can be active in the midst of all disturbances, of all absorptions; it is with us in the world, through social exigences, in the interior of the family, in the solitude of the home, in work and in rest, in the ordinary actions of life and even on a bed of pain, through depression and insomnia.

2nd. The life of union with God alone gives life to exercises of piety.

We are often distracted in them, preoccupied; the movement of the mouth is wasted and the heart is far. We feel, alas! that all this has but one *body*, that animation is not felt. But the *soul* has the habit of the presence of God, and with this soul it is impossible that the heart should not act more frequently and should not occasionally vivify our exterior practices.

Ladies, the world has *volatized salts, concentrated spirits;* they are carried in portable vials of which you know the name.

Weak temperaments often inhale them to prevent exhaustions of nature, or to calm vertigos. *Strong* temperaments use them as well, when the air becomes heavy, hot and vitiated.

Permit me, Ladies, in finishing, to present you with a divine *vial*, where all the *evangelical* salt is found, marvelously concentrated with all its virtue, it is the Gospel itself which our Lord has *reduced* to the eight beatitudes.

Inhale often, inhale always the *salt* of these beatitudes, for constitutions are weak, vertigos frequent, the nervous system very much irritated by the things of earth; for the air of the world which you breathe is warm in every way, it effects the heart, too often it is vitiated.

In the folly of expenditure, and in the flash of jewels, go inhale this salt, Ladies: "Blessed are the poor in spirit; blessed are the merciful!"[1]

In the assaults of dress, of success, of vanity, of rivalry, inhale this salt: "Blessed are the meek and humble!"

In noisy pleasures, in temptations that captivate, inhale this salt: "Blessed are they that mourn; blessed are they that hunger and thirst after justice!"

First of all in your dress; then in certain eccentric steps, finally in those delicate occasions where evil enters by the large door of vanity, inhale this salt: "Blessed are the pure of heart!"

What shall I say in those moments when we must prefer the peace of God beyond all else, when the world smiles and whispers at our simplicity and our reserve? Ah! in these moments inhale quickly this salt: "Blessed are the peacemakers; blessed are they that suffer persecution for justice's sake!"

Ladies, if to each trial of the life of the world and the family, you would oppose one of the eight beatitudes well inhaled; if you would take this

[1] Matt., v., 3–10.

practice as the element of union with God, what perfection there would soon be in your christian life, and how sweet, noble and worthy this life would be, if in your *walks* you *would walk* with the Lord!

THE EXERCISE OF PRAYER AND MEDITATION.

Omni tempore orantes.
"Pray without ceasing." I Thess., v, 17.

THE life of union with God, which is practised by recalling His holy presence and by the frequent elevation of the heart towards the things of heaven, is the extension, the continuation, the supplement and the vivification of prayer properly speaking.

It is this life which fills the precept: "Pray without ceasing." You must pray, pray always, without ceasing. It was this life of union which made St. Augustine say: "Prayer is continual when our fervour is continual. *Multa est precatio, ubi fervens perseverat intentio.*"

But this *brook* which never tarries, would dry up if we did not feed it at certain hours, by recurring to the principal *source*, which is positive prayer, express meditation. It is well then to draw from this source in the retreat, and to speak of *prayer and meditation.*

Prayer! Hackneyed subject, which perhaps grieves you when it is announced from the pulpit, because every one is fully edified on this subject. I am going to try to present it to you with some interest.

I do not intend to speak to you here:

Of the *dignity of prayer*, which is the exclusive privilege of the dignity of man, and which alone constitutes him king and priest of creation;

Of the *natural facility of prayer*, which man knows perfectly well how to prostitute to obtain the material things of earth, success in business, places, and passions even, bending himself before the power which can give, going down on his knees before idols of the flesh;

Of *the necessity of prayer*, to render glory and homage to God, to solicit the graces of salvation, to obtain secondarily the goods of time;

Of the conditions of prayer, respect, humility, confidence, perseverance.

These are the elements of religious instruction.

In a retreat, it is more appropriate to give useful advice on the *nature of prayer*, and that is the favour I am going to ask of your pious attention.

THE NATURE OF PRAYER.

Prayer or meditation is the elevation of the mind and the heart to God, to offer Him our duties, to expose to Him our needs, and to become better for His glory: *ascensio mentis ad Deum.*

This word: *ascension of the soul to God,* reproves and repudiates the first thing those prayers born of the lips; this play of the organs which only modifies the air with vain sounds, and agitates the mouth through routtine, without any attention to the words articulated. Unless this movement of the lips (owing to the weakness of the soul), be still a last concussion, a prolonged undulation of a movement of the heart, which becomes heavy, grows fatigued, and falls.

But prayer, at least in its principle, its preparation, or its first intention, supposes a contact, a commerce of the soul with God, a holy frequentation of thought and will with the Lord.

And with this just definition, already prayer seems to me to be the mysterious key of all religion. It is that which accustoms us to detach ourselves from earth, to raise ourselves above created objects, to understand that there is a good, an interest above all the goods and interests here below. It is the *sursum corda*, "the heart raised" put in practice. I cannot thus put myself in contact, in relation, in commerce, in frequentation with God, without recognizing now His sovereign domain, now my duties towards Him, now the gratitude I owe to His benefits, now the need I have of His continual assistance; asking pardon for the wrong and evil of sin, without appreciating it fully. Prayer contains all that religion teaches, all it promises, all it commands, all it wishes to have avoided; and in a contact, where we *frequent* God, the result is to become like Him, and to succeed little by little in being just, good and perfect like Him.

On the contrary, without prayer, or what amounts to the same thing, with the routine and mechanical movement alone of the lips, the soul crawls here below and one flies but heavily in moments of danger; the soul vegetates and sinks deeper and deeper into the things of earth. While with real prayer, causing the mind and heart to *mount* to God, the soul soars in the regions of good, lives by truth, justice and peace. It sees the things of the world through the prism of heaven which decomposes them, and frees the occupations of earth of all that is impure, unjust, disorderly, opposed to the holiness of God and real happiness.

Just as the water of the sea, lifted into vapour by the sun, filters through the great apparel of the atmosphere, and frees itself in that marvelous alembic, to be distilled into sweet savoury water, in passing over various strata in the heart of the mountains; just as the affairs, works, cares, dangers, sorrows and corruption even of terrestial life, when lifted up by the fervour and grace of prayer, lose in that ascension all that is hard, material, bitter, corrupted in them, and return to mix themselves more holily with the various occupations of life.

But the heart and the mind do not rise thus towards God in meditation in a vague manner without an end. It is not a philosophical consideration, a theory of admiration and gratitude, a dry study of the things of God, a sensible and natural movement of the heart as towards created objects, prayer and its *elevation* has a more exalted and a more practical end.

I.

First, there must be the elevation of both the heart and the mind to God at the same time.

Hence separation from terrestrial things by keeping the senses contained and recollected; and separation from the senses themselves by keeping the soul still more recollected.

Hence perfect recollection of the soul, which shuts out everything, and of the senses in which it is tangled; which *recollects* its strength scattered here and there on the things of this earth.

Hence, gentle religious attention, without contention, without restraint, and in this state real contact with God, union of fervour, of desire and of love.

May be you find this too difficult, even impossible, still it is found in souls the least accustomed to prayer. I do not wish to speak of those states where the heart, captivated by terrestrial passions, by worldly interests, finds itself drawn of its own accord far from creatures, to enter into perfect recollection which concentrates all its strength on one single object; you will say that that is the energy of passion and that prayer has something more calm and less absorbing in it. I shall only speak to you of two instances where prayer obtains its marvelous elevation, its absolute recollection in over-burdened souls; in certain moments filled with joy, effusion and gratitude, and in pressing need or sharp grief. In these moments the mind and the heart are so united to God, that men take occasion from this not to care to pray excepting when they can speak thus; pretending by affection for these fugitive movements, to justify their withdrawal from regular and regulated prayer.

"When I pray, they say, it is with all my heart and without formula; formula only serves to bother and cool."

"With all the heart;" that is very good, only it is too rare, and too reserved for interested circumstances. Without giving always effusions of the soul which do not depend on us, it would be well to vivify salutary formulas, by using them justly, to aid us in the contact with God.

In virtue of this elevation of the heart which is essential to meditation, I should prefer short to overburdening prayers, slow and heartfelt prayers to precipitation. I should like public prayer with the singing which accompanies it, because singing *gives the time* to feel and to express; in the singing of the Psalms for instance, there is just time to feel and breathe the perfume, and if one is bored, it is because he feels nothing. Try to recite the Lord's Prayer or the Hail Mary in this way in union with God, and you will taste what elevation, attraction, sweetness and profit prayer has; without this enlivening spirit, I conceive, without excusing it, the dislike for formulas, their insufficiency, and the ennui of public prayer.

II.

The first object of prayer should be to *render our duties to God*.

Prayer is not the consecration of a certain religious egoism. It is the *link* of the soul with God, and of souls together; in it we should occupy ourselves *more* with God than with ourselves; with others *as much* as with ourselves.

It is a *duty* to render our duties to God; to adore Him, to praise Him, to bless Him, to glorify Him, to give Him thanks.

Besides, it is a *means* to conciliate divine favours for ourselves. See in the prayers of the earth, of man to man, of poor to rich, of little to great, of the destitute to the powerful, there is a certain repulsion if we think that people only come to us for themselves; but if they consider us, we feel at once inclined to accord them their wishes. The prayer of this earth has also found the assured and secret road to the heart, when it has had the instinct to commence by praising and blessing the heart which it solicits.

Our Lord has admirably sanctioned this end in the prayer which He has taught us: the beginning is laudative, He exalts the power of God; the three first petitions bless the name of God, the reign of God, the will of God, before asking Him for the daily bread, the pardon of offences, the deliverance from temptation and evil. And again, the Church in her prayers has imitated this charitable mode, we ask for all: "Give us, forgive us, deliver us."

The principal reason why public worship is accompanied with so much *ennui*, believe me, is not always owing to its length, that is only the exterior excuse; the secret reason is, that it seems to us that in it one occupies oneself *too much* with God, a *great deal* with others and everything, and *not enough* with self.

But we must accustom ourselves to the duty and even the happiness of occupying ourselves with God, and find it sweet to sing: "Praise ye the name of the Lord! We that live, bless the Lord."[1] And if we return to our particular preoccupations or our personal sorrows, let us try to absorb them in the merit of the common and general prayer, to bury them in those words which answer everything: "Have mercy on us, receive our prayers."

III.

The second object of prayer is *to expose our needs to God*. Here we *happily* return to ourselves, for this personal interest is not excluded, only it must be in place: God first and above all, then ourselves

[1] Psalm CXIII, 1–18.

and our neighbour. "Seek ye therefore first the kingdom of God," at least by appreciation; seek first the justice and the fidelity which lead to this kingdom. "And all these things shall be added unto you."[1] Then, when our Lord gives us the order of even our personal demands, what harmony, what condescension for our weakness.

The first thing, the daily bread, the material needs and necessities, for fear that if our hearts are preoccupied and weighed down by the solicitudes of earth, they will not be easily raised to the things of God. Then the pardon of our sins, the evil and misfortune of which we feel the more when we are freed from the anxieties of life. Then the deliverance from temptation which would produce a guilty future. Finally, the withdrawal of all evil, of the sovereign evil, and of those evils which often lead us far from God, and make us neglect His grace.

If we ask *in the name of all*, do not let us be afraid; it is surely to our best interest not to speak in the name of our poor individuality, God being touched with our charity for our brethren, and forgetting our personal indignity, covered by the

[1] Matt., VI, 33.

merits of others; will it be well, then, I ask, to fix the gaze of the Lord too intently on our isolated misery?

IV.

The result of prayer is *to become better*, and that for the glory of God.

This progressive amelioration is the natural effect of prayer in general, since there is frequentation, contact with God. It is the effect of prayer on the whole of the day, the contrary would be distressing, and would sometimes go as far as scandal. It is above all the effect of the great prayer of Sunday, in assisting at the Holy Sacrifice, a prayer which should have sufficient energy, grace and influence to ameliorate the week that is to follow.

But this very desirable effect will only be truly and abundantly produced by the prayer called *meditation*. We pray in vain, we read in vain, we listen in vain, if we do not meditate; but do not be frightened if I wish to make women of *meditation* of you.

1st. Take the resolution to make at least a quarter of an hour of meditation each morning.

2nd. Make it from any book you wish, consulting your taste, your attraction, that which speaks to your heart; the Psalms, the Gospel, the Imitation, the Lives of the Saints, and the other books of practical meditation; they are the source.

3rd. Divide this meditation into three parts: one for the *beginning;* that is the presence of God, the regret of your faults in His presence, the invocation of the lights and graces of the Holy Ghost. One for the *body* of the meditation; that is attention to the subject, reflection on the subject, and the application which you make of it to yourself. One for the *conclusion;* that is, the special and practical resolutions, a good thought to keep during the day, and the prayer which terminates it.

Ah! here is a great and excellent way to be united to God, to profit by the life of union, to enliven this union with God by the Sacraments.

THE LIFE OF SELF-DENIAL.

> *Tantum proficies, quantum tibi ipsi vim intuleris. Amen.* (*Imitat.*, liv. I, ch. *XXV.*)
> "You will advance only in proportion as you do violence to yourself."
> Amen.

LADIES, I borrow this text from the Imitation; it is nothing more than the practical deduction of this oracle of Jesus Christ: "If any one will come after me, let him deny himself."[1]

Have you ever seen them construct a vault or an arch, the arch of a bridge? They begin by placing the perpendicular bases; this work is easy—it is only necessary to find solid ground, and to place stone on stone in regular order. But when the work reaches the point where the construction is to leave the perpendicular to commence the curved line, the difficulty becomes serious. First, they outline the arch or vault with strong pieces of

[1] Matt., xvi, 24.

frame-work that rest on the secured bases; right and left they place simultaneously the stones that are to form the centre: these stones are called *arch-stones;* they rest on the frame-work, but will not be united until the last stone of the middle, the key of the arch is put in, which will give the strength of union to all the *arch-stones;* then they take out the supports, and the arch acquires all its solidity, precisely by the weight with which they load it. But if the centre lacked this angular stone, this key of the arch, no matter how carefully it was constructed the whole would fall in, because no stone would be united to a central force.

So it is, Ladies, with this edification, this building of God, of which we are the subject: *Dei aedificatio estis.* In vain we raise wisely all these *arch-stones* which we call the *regulated* life, the *useful* life, the life of *union with God*, the life of meditation; in vain is all this retraced, joined and cemented by the most fervent exercises, the most holy practices; if the key of the arch is lacking, if the life of *self-denial* is wanting, all falls to pieces and the work is lost: *In vanum laboraverunt qui aedificant.* And the Lord gave this order to Ezechiel: "Say to them that daub without tempering, that it (the wall) shall fall;" so this mixture, this *temper* of the virtues, is the renouncement of self, abnegation.

There is nothing but abnegation in all that has preceded; the love of God is the renunciation of our self-love; the flight of the world, the renunciation of our intoxicating allurements; the regulated life, the sacrifice of our inconstancy; the useful life is the sacrifice of our lazy fancies; the life of union with God, is the sacrifice of our dissipations. But if we do not make use of the main spring and the constant movement of all this machinery, we have done nothing; it is for this reason that we must crown the work by the *life of the habit of conquering self*.

Here is another comparison which will render this essential truth palpable to you; it is taken from the Holy Scriptures:

"The hand of the Lord," said Ezechiel, "was upon me, and brought me forth in the spirit of the Lord, and set me down in the midst of a plain that was full of bones.[1]

[1] Ezechiel, XXXVII, 1, 3, 4, 5, 7, 8, 9, 10.

"And He said to me: 'Son of man dost thou think these bones shall live?' And I answered Him: 'O Lord God thou knowest.'

"And He said to me: 'Prophesy concerning these bones, and say to them: Ye dry bones hear the word of the Lord:'

"Thus saith the Lord God to these bones: 'Behold I will send my spirit into you, and you shall live.'

"And I prophesied as He had commanded me: and as I prophesied, there was a noise and behold a commotion and the bones came together each one to its joint.

"And I saw, and behold the sinews and the flesh came up upon them; and the skin was stretched out over them, but there was no spirit in them.

"And He said to me: 'Prophesy to the spirit, prophesy, O Son of Man, and say to the spirit:' Thus saith the Lord: 'Come spirit, from the four winds, and blow upon these slain and let them live again.'

"And I prophesied as He had commanded me: and the spirit came into them and they lived; and they stood up upon their feet, an exceeding great army."

The application is easy. Those bones which approach their joints represent the soul approaching God who is its centre and its life. Those nerves, that flesh, that skin which spread themselves over the bones, are the forces and the virtues that come to sustain divine love and to prepare life. But real life, that life which keeps everything in its place, which communicates the strength to stand up and walk with animation, and is the fertile breath of christian renunciation, of which I am about to speak to you.

I.

The first principle which we must imprint deeply on our souls is, that self-love, egoism, self-seeking is the greatest enemy of good; it is that which ruins everything, under all its forms; in the individual, it is a principle of individual death; in the public man, it is a principle of general destruction. Abnegation is the enemy of self-love; it alone can suppress, neutralize and destroy it.

But here is the world proclaiming immediately and pretending that self-love is the main spring of woman's virtue, that it is that which gives her the indefatigable energy for good.

Drive away this injurious axiom, Ladies; it will change the nature of all that is most innate, most delicate in your souls, devotion; and because the principle is *injurious*, you have the right to conclude that it is *unjust*.

The world recoils at this answer, and hides some orbs of its interweaving; it affirms in an undertone that a *little* self-love is necessary, that it is, if not the base, at least the necessary prop to your weakness. Listen: when the digestion is chronically slow, by defect or irritation of the organs, the injection, even in small doses, of spirituous excitants, or burning aromas calm for a moment and precipitate the work; but the organic trouble grows in a distressing way; that is the effect of a little self-love on weak virtue. Instead of this remedy, which exasperates the organism, the doctor seeing that inflammation is the cause of the trouble, quickly forbids the pretended stimulants, and prescribes diet and bitters; that is to say all this *physical abnegation* tempers and restores to the normal condition; and when this condition is renewed, stimulants should be employed; but never pretended stimulants. That is the effect of moral renouncement and abnegation.

Come, says the world, a great deal of abnegation, but a little grain of self-love; it is an incentive which can do no harm! The smallest dose is too much. All the same, the physician yields before certain sick fancies which cannot do much harm, and if you hold absolutely to curing *likes with likes* (which is a mistake in morals) do not forget that in this system the doses should be *infinitesimal;* or rather, return to the evangelical method, to its *abnegation* which cures contraries by contraries; it is the surest and most efficacious way to sustain virtues.

II.

In spite of this vivifying principle, the life of abnegation, of sacrifice, of the habit of conquering self is what is most lacking *in all christian lives*.

It is what was lacking in the first education; it is what is wanting in that *great education* with which religion embraces our life from the cradle to the grave.

When the principle of abnegation has not been deposited in the hearts of men, they become egoists, are despised outside and are intolerable at home.

But it concerns you, Ladies, so I ask you what is the education of woman in general with regard to renouncement? I speak of *education*, which I distinguish essentially from *instruction*; the latter is pushed very far and leaves nothing to be desired; nothing but moderation, adorned with solidity and modesty.

So I say that your education has been defective, wanting, nearly worthless.

It consisted for you, and will consist for your children and your children's children in two principles, which are:

Nothing to conquer self.

Everything to concentrate self on self.

See:

1st. Woman is a *creature of duty*, and of the gravest duty; she is the *help* given to man to direct him in his joys, to sustain him in his depressions, to enlighten him even in his business; she is the *mother* of man, to whom she should communicate a broad, healthy, strong life; she is the only instructress of the children, there is no education if it does not take its source from the heart of a mother; so they raise this woman like a doll, they do not even punish her like a doll! The first lesson of virtue which she heard and which she retained well, was a lesson of egoism and personal interest; she is promised *a pretty dress* if she is very good, quiet and obedient. Later she is directed only by gross appetite, frivolous vanity, ascribing all to self; and still later, all has been said when she has been taught to wear a lace on her gown, or a flower in her hat with a certain grace.

2nd. Woman is a *creature of suffering;* it is the lot of her physical life, too often the portion of her social life. And they make a soft, heedless, negligent, indolent creature of her, a creature who thinks herself full of grace in an abandon without strength or vigour. To initiate her into a long life of privations, they stuff her with happiness, make her childhood up by depriving her of nothing, and have her make the apprenticeship of a life of sacrifices by keeping from her the smallest contradictions. We see mothers and christian mothers, who adopt as a principle that children must be happy; the poor little things! and that they should be formed by the most insipid spoiling for a life which will always ask for the energy of abnegation! So how can you expect these little ones, incapable of understanding, of guessing the secret of your maternal amends, not to become accustomed to look upon themselves as *little centres* where all must meet; to say to themselves: "The world, it is I; others, it is I: or rather, others are nothing, there is nothing but me!"

3rd. Woman is a *creature of subjection and dependence*. It is in vain for her to say, to act, to pose in her utopias and her dreams as queen of the world, as conqueror of society, as vanquisher of man; it is in vain for her to take the wrong view of the homages which civilization confers on her, and to confound a gracious concession with a rigorous right; woman is by her nature and by her destiny a dependent being, who should be submissive. So her mother, blind in her tenderness, has made a little divinity of her; first her idol, than an idol destined to be sought after, fêted, served and adored in the world. From this those affected, pretentious, and sometimes imperious and haughty manners;

from this that high decided and cutting voice, when it is not ridiculously soft and delicate; from this that ungraceful self-possession, those airs of a woman when they are still only girls, that push which enstalls itself without ceremony on seats that are not destined for youth; finally, that pose which seems to say by each movement, each look, each inflection of the voice, "All is due to me." Poor women, they would have so much grace if they only knew that devotion is their life, submission their atmosphere; if they loved to forget self, if they had the happy instinct to drape themselves in the simplicity of sweet modesty!

III.

Do you wish to remedy all these disorders, which draw after them so many sorrows in life? You will only succeed by christian abnegation.

Mothers, put abnegation in your hearts; for it is *self* you love, it is *self* you admire, it is *self* you praise and produce in your children; it is *substitution of self-love*.

Inspire this abnegation in your children (both boys and girls), even in *words* and in *nothings*. Be careful about this, for in the education of the young words are things, nothings are affairs. The exaggerated appreciation of a futile detail of dress is not indifferent; it has often prepared the mind for the false, the heart for indolence, life for trifles. For you this nothing is a nothing, this detail is a detail, because you know already how to appreciate life; for the child, this nothing is a complete preoccupation that absorbs her thoughts and her desires.

Do not put instruction alone in the education without making it loved; work without engaging the heart in it; religious practices without revealing their spirit and their end; words of honour which slur over the interest of egoism; put in it above all, virtue as courage, the necessity of conquering self, the respect of duty before all else.

Take this idea in well, Ladies: that your education should be going on all during life, that it will not finish until the perfect age of eternity; that it rests on self-denial, that abnegation is the only strength of the soul, is the main spring of all virtue.

Inspire it in your children : in the boys, by the idea of duty; in the girls, by the idea of devotion.

Try each day to conquer self in some one thing, and each evening to account for one victory which you have gained over self; without that *you have lost your day*.

IV.

Do not think that this great life of self-denial is only a detail, a detached page from *Chesterfield;* that it is only a means like any other to succeed in the world, and to appear to advantage and with grace in it. Abnegation is the whole man—perhaps still more, the whole woman.

The Romans had no other word to express *virtue* than the term *courage*, because virtue is always a courageous violence done to corrupted nature.

Antique wisdom divined the Gospel, when it gave these two great words that include all, to its adepts as a motto : Abstain and sustain : *Abstine et sustine*.

But self-denial has never been more sanctioned than by the Gospel.

"If any man will come after Me," said Jesus Christ, "let him deny himself, and take up his cross and follow Me."[1]

"Denying," says St. Paul, "ungodliness and worldly desires, we should live soberly and justly and godly in this world."[2]

And the author of the Imitation, making echo, proclaims this immortal truth: "The greater *violence* that thou offereth thyself the greater progress thou wilt make."

At the same time, do not forget that there is happiness in this abnegation, perhaps the only happiness we can taste here below; for to renounce self, is to renounce a thousand causes for grief, is to spare oneself a thousand sorrows: and to suffer in the abnegation of a christian heart, is to greatly soften the sorrows that we must always carry, and that become exasperated in the lacerations of egoism.

---

[1] Matt., xvi, 24. [2] Titus, ii, 12.

THE CHRISTIAN MISSION OF WOMEN.

> *Ego sanctifico meipsum, ut sint et ipsi sanctificati in veritate.*
> "I sanctify myself, that they also may be sanctified in truth." John, XVII, 19.

TO SANCTIFY oneself in order that others may be sanctified, that, Ladies, is the rule established by Jesus Christ; and if you are to pour a stream of good example in the world, you must absolutely pour from plenitude.

So you have to spread and to shower a great deal. God has given you a mission; and it is for this reason, that you cannot love God, fly from the world, profit by grace, penetrate yourselves with prayer, exercise yourselves to a regulated useful life united to God and nurtured by abnegation, to too great an extent.

I wish, then, in the last place, and as a crowning to this retreat to speak to you of the christian mission of woman.

When God makes souls for the apostleship, he forms them of *abnegation* and *devotion*, we cannot conceive of an *apostle* without these two virtues which strip him of self, to make him give self to the service of others.

So, whoever has studied the nature of woman, recognizes in her a heart that God has created to renounce itself and to devote itself. Abnegation with all its energy of sacrifice and devotion, with all its delicacy of charity, constitutes the special character of woman; it is her instinct, her dignity, her grandeur, her empire, her strength, her wealth and her grace.

From whence I conclude that God has destined woman for an *apostleship*, and that under the reign of the Gospel, which has re-established her so gloriously, she has a christian mission to fill.

We must examine the height of this mission, and the vast field over which it exercises itself.

In the thought of God, the Creator, woman was made as a *help* for man, she was given to him as an aid, as a charm placed by the side of his labours: *Faciamus ei adjutorium.* This help is not only material, we must understand it in the elevated order of a mission; we must read in it some traits of that thought of St. Paul: "We are God's coadjutors," we help him to save souls: "*Dei sumus adjutores.*"[1]

God created woman *like unto man;* he did not draw her from clay, he formed her of the body of Adam, from one of his ribs. He did not draw her from the feet of man, says St. Thomas, because she was not destined to be his slave; he did not draw her from his head, because she was not to rule or command; he drew her from the side, near the heart, because she was to be an equal, a companion, a being who was to love and to devote herself. Also when this new creature, from the hands of God, is presented to Adam, he declares at the sight of her, that she is *bone of his bone, flesh of his flesh,* and he accepts her as *a companion given to him.*

There is the work of God—let us see the work of sin.

Sin commenced by woman; it is by her that we all are born, that we all die.

Her condemnation also is terrible; discomfort and infirmity shall be her life; she shall become

[1] I Cor., III, 9.

mother only through pain, and in the midst of perils; and she shall be under the power of man. This subjection is not a simple article of our code, a law made by man, a right of the strongest; it is an oracle from the mouth of God, an irrevocable sentence pronounced by the Supreme Judge: *Et eris sub potestate viri.*

This subjection which is the consequence, the sorrow and the seal of the original degradation, takes tremendous proportions under the empire of sin. It goes as far as the degradation of the creature and of personality; plurality in the most revolting polygamy; assimilation to the animals which man can keep, establishment of *things* and the destruction of *person; slavery,* the children of which are nothing more than *products.* With idolatrous peoples, this slavery bends the woman in an unworthy manner; and even among the Jewish people her servitude is terribly degrading.

It will only be at the end of forty centuries that this noble, delicate and devoted creature will be re-established by Jesus Christ, with the reparation of sin, and the work will still be long through the times of grace.

But after having carried the seal of sin so long, woman is to bear the seal of redemption; she is going to take her rank again, and remount to her place with glory. For here now is the work of reparatory grace.

The new Legislator has struck a great blow; by a word He leads things back to their first origin: *Ab initio non fuit sic.* He banishes polygamy and orders the unity of marriage, *erunt duo in carne una.* All reparation was in this single point.

Without unity of marriage, woman is a thing of poor value, that man would multiply as his lands and his beasts of burden. With unity of marriage, she is a precious creature beyond comparison, who alone can suffice for the help and charm of a whole life.

Without the indissolubility of marriage, woman is a thing of vile price that one can take, leave, or take back, according to the whims of the estimation, according to the fancies and the caprices of the heart. Indissoluble marriage, such as God has re-established it, consecrates the dignity of a creature whom one cannot take lightly, or ever throw aside, because God has united her to man; has not abandoned her to his inconstancy, and has judged her worthy of an eternal union. Under this legislation God presents woman to man as possessing sufficient riches of heart to hold his taste forever; and not to be compared with any other possession, which he changes at his fancy: *Quod Deus conjunxit, homo non separet.*

But in this one and indissoluble marriage, it was still necessary to re-establish the equilibrium of rights and duties; two words are going to put all in marvellous harmony. Man who has the authority, should love, *viri, diligite;* he should be neither a despot, an egoist, nor indifferent; he should love. Woman should be submissive, *mulieres subditae sint*: she should be submissive with affection. The power of man *should stoop* by love, work and devotion. The dependence of woman should rise by the ascendancy of her sweetness, by the dignity of devoted virtue, and all would equalize itself on a common *level*.

At the same time it was not sufficient to re-establish the central point of the rehabilitation; the balance had leaned too long and too powerfully on the man's side, it was necessary to give a powerful push from the other side.

God the Saviour also wished to be born of a woman, to be made of a woman, as says St. Paul, of a woman fully re-established, coming from the hands of God a thousand times more pure than Eve, of a woman who had no share in original sin. He is born of a virgin mother, full of grace, blessed among all women, that all generations shall proclaim blessed. This woman is Mary, the new Eve, the real mother of the living, the glory of all the daughters of Adam, the arch type of the reinstated woman.

Again, in His public ministry, if Jesus Christ walks preceded by His disciples, escorted by His apostles, He is followed by women who serve Him with their goods and their devotion.

Again, His miraculous power extends itself equally to the one and the other sex; He cures the son of the officer, and the daughter of the chananeen. He receives the prodigal son and the adulterous woman, and His friendship honours Martha and Mary, as well as Lazarus and John; finally, on the Cross, it is His mother whom He gives us for our mother in the order of grace: *Mulier, ecce filius tuus.*

The horizon of the rehabilitation of woman grows still larger. At the foot of the Cross there are only Mary and the beloved disciple; the other apostles have flown, but they are replaced on Calvary by the faithful women who followed the Saviour in His evangelical journeys. For the cares of the Sepulchre, they are nearly alone; also on the day of Resurrection, Jesus Christ raises them to a sort of apostleship. He appears first to Mary Magdalene, then to the holy women, and it is they whom He chooses to proclaim His triumph over death: "And going quickly, tell ye His disciples that He is risen; and behold He will go before you into Galilee."[1] Finally, these witnesses, these heralds, these apostles of the Resurrection, persevered with the disciples until the day of Pentecost; they are found in the cenacle under the guide and care of Mary; they are named before the brothers; all, women and men, are filled with the Holy Ghost.

These women at the cenacle were there as the deputation of their sex. It was in this home of love and devotion that their hearts, created in the spirit of sacrifice, received a new creation, and drew

[1] Matt., xxviii, 7.

for themselves and their successors the excellent *genius* of charity, as St. Paul calls it. From thence those women-apostles who accompanied the apostles, after having accompanied Jesus Christ; from thence that luminous train of charitable zeal that extends from Paola and Marcella, Clotilde and Blanche, Chantal and Longueville to our days, and which will last until the end of time.

This is why the respectful consideration of a sort of *worship* has surrounded women in christian civilization; it is because religion has placed the triple crown of woman, wife and mother on her brow; the triple crown due to weakness, suffering and devotion. Also on the day which consecrates the new era of religious civilization, on the triumphant day of Easter, the Church sends forth an unusual cry of joy which re-establishes the entire equilibrium: " O sons and daughters, praise ye the Lord!" " *O filii et filiae* . . . . *Alleluia!* "

But, Ladies, duties are always in proportion to rights and gifts. Much is asked of him to whom much has been given—greatness imposes great cares. We are exalted only to serve and to devote ourselves. If then I have placed the foundation of your elevation and your greatness, it is to tell you that you have a *christian mission*, and a high apostleship to fill.

II.

This apostleship of woman should be exercised in the family, in the world, and in religion.

But let us say quickly, Ladies, let us say as a general rule, before making any application, that if this word *apostleship* charms the ear of the heart agreeably because it seems to open a vast field to the activity which it excites, to a little domination which is to exercise itself under the shade of the good to be done; this *apostleship* must be understood in all the reserve of order, calm, simplicity and modesty; and above all in religious matters, where the faithful, whoever they may be, should only follow, serve and aid; must be understood with all reserve of dependence on the legitimate authority which should direct.

1st. The apostleship of woman in the family by a spirit of obedience and subjection. This dependence, full of dignity, in the wise and reasonable woman, is a sweet and gentle preaching. Your yoke, Ladies, is *dragged* with exhausting fatigue, you cannot shake it off without being murdered by it, but it is *worn* with dignity, and sometimes with happiness. Your task is sufficiently beautiful; by the obedience of the heart you will rise to the level and the equality of rights; what am I saying? You will reign: to reign is a legitimate and regular right. Domination is always contestable and exposed to storms. Besides, you have only to take the part of holy obedience to bring men to religion, your silence is the preaching which wins them, according to this oracle of the apostle: "Let women be subject to their husbands, so that those who do not believe in the divine word may be won to God, without words, by the conduct of their wives."[1]

Finally, obedience is the only sceptre becoming to your delicate fingers; any other will weigh you down because it is too heavy, or else will prick your hand because it is a reed. The affectation of independence makes you ridiculous, and only serves to subject you the more. "I know of nothing more ridiculous," said a man of experience, "than a

[1] I Peter, III, 1.

woman who *commands;* unless it be—a man who *obeys."*

Inspire your daughters with this spirit, instead of exalting them with unjust pretensions. Do not let them form a wrong impression of the respect with which their sex is surrounded. Destroy this disastrous principle in them : " That everything is *due* to woman, that woman owes nothing, that everything should cede to her." Finally, bring them up in obedience and for obedience, if you wish to rear them in the order of nature, for their happiness, and for their mission.

Apostleship by the angelic spirit of serenity and consolation.

Woman is not a tempest, she is a rainbow in the midst of stormy clouds. The strength of woman is in her exhaustless sweetness, in her calm, which governs agitated situations; it is by that, that Clotildes and Monicas gain their husbands and their sons; man, when he comes back to the Lord, wants to come to the God of a Clotilde, the son wants to come back to the God whom his mother adores.

Be also angels of prayer and religious exercises in your family, it belongs to you to retain the blessing of heaven on the domestic hearths, and to preserve the fidelity of all to religion. From how many homes would worship have disappeared were in not for woman!

Apostleship, by the education of the children.

It is you, Ladies, who are the only teachers of childhood, the *first* catechists, and it is not without reason that the expression: "*to drink in piety with our mother's milk,*" has become established.

You were not yet mothers, and already you offered to God the fruit of your womb, you begged the Lord to bless it, to let it reach christian regeneration. If the health and temperament of the mother influence the organism of the child, we can assure ourselves without fear, that the sentiments of her soul, and her piety communicate themselves also to this soul newly created to animate a body.

As soon as your child appeared to light, you blessed it before kissing it, and when they brought it back to you from the baptismal font, your benedictions were still more tender and more intense.

He understood nothing, this child, and each day you marked his forehead with the sign of the cross, you even made him express it mechanically by guiding his little hand.

As soon as he could open his eyes, to know and smile at you, you took him to Mary's altar. There, this little one saw a woman like you, who held a child like him in her arms, and that was the first light of religion for him.

As soon as the child could lisp, your knees were his first *prie Dieu;* sweet position where one kneels on a mother's lap, resting on her heart! Finally, it was at your feet that he received the first elements of catechism, and that you taught him to fear and love the good *God*, impressed those two words of the highest philosophy on him—that God sees everything, that He is all good ; and that we are on this earth to know, love and serve Him, and by this means to reach life eternal. Sweet catechism, that we never forget, so gentle and sweet is its remembrance!

Why is it that you will not follow this happy education? Why change all at once, this sweet culture into distressing idolatry? Why this idolatry for children who lose you and who lose themselves ; who first of all blind you, give you eyes not to see, ears not to hear, a mouth not to talk; who soon reduce your authority to a timid prayer, and finish by making you tremble before the idol? This idolatry weakens your heart so, that the faults of the idol grow to excess and make it insupportable to all others but yourself. "Love one another," said a man of wit, in leaving an unbearable people, "for if you do not, I do not know who will love you." Your weakness, Ladies, has made your children such that one can say to you with regret: "Love them well for yourselves and for others, for you alone will be able to stand them, and without you who will love them."

I have often wondered where that maternal idolatry came from which has sprung up in the present generation. I have asked myself whether the heart of a mother had acquired all at once a development, an expansion, a strength unknown to generations which have preceded us.

Nature could not change her gait to this extent. A mother's heart has always been what it is, God has not formed it again and made it over for our times. A mother's heart has always been an ocean of tenderness, affection, help, compassion, devotion, indulgence and love. But this ocean had a boundary like the physical ocean; they said to it: "You shall come so far," but the ocean of the maternal heart has tried to overstep its limits.

Its strength was so great, that God gave her counterpoises; they were in the love of the Creator, well above the love of the creature, the most dear; in the conjugal love which would draw a part of the love, in the heart of a husband; in a sweet and reverential fear of the ruling passions less pronounced in the faults of childhood; in the more serious thought of the education and the future, of the dearest beings; finally, they were in that great responsibility that inspired Blanche of Castile with an immortal word: "My Son, God knows how much I love you! Nevertheless, I would prefer to see you deprived of your kingdom and of life, than to know that you were stained with sin!"

I do not know, Ladies, whether these counterpoises exist any longer; I do not know whether love has flown from the wife's and daughter's heart, to throw itself entirely into the mother's heart, and from thence to engulf the child's heart to overflowing; I do not know if the respect for others is weakened, if the seriousness of christian customs is destroyed;

but if it were so, I should no longer be astonished at this flood of idolatry; I could understand the ravages of this torrent which nothing checks.

2nd. Apostleship of the woman in the world.

Your mission in the world, Ladies, does not consist in preaching and governing by a certain reformatory right that your virtue will give you. St. Paul is positive on this point. "But I suffer not a woman to teach, nor to use authority over the man; but to be in silence."[1] And if obedience and sweetness constitutes the preaching of woman in the family, modesty and reserve will be her powerful edification in the world.

A woman who wishes to fill her mission on this point, will avoid above all, boasting about the respect and regard which she receives. This point is essential, it is the exordium of your preaching, and the exordium should be simple, modest and insinuating. The audience flies in a passion at every orator who poses with triumphant and presuming airs.

Reaching a certain age (if one ever does reach it), woman should avoid revenging herself of it by a

[1] I Tim., 12.

critical mind, an imperious air, a cutting and domineering tone.

At every age, she should avoid the boast of science, the ridicule of the abused woman, who at bottom is only the incomprehensible woman.

And when she has, by force of modesty, disposed minds and hearts to listen to her, a sweet word, well placed, will be her apostleship, and will make now virtue, now the reputation of others, now the rules of morality respected.

A useful word, always gentle, and never accentuated by a doctrinal tone should blame irreligion, the duel, improper dressing, disorderly pleasures, and the weakness of spoiling children without limit.

When it is question of religion, she should apply herself to make it sweet and gentle in her person, by a great and modest indulgence; then by her words, showing only the sweetness, the interest and the happiness that are attached to it.

She should fortify this savoury religious influence, by never saying any harm of her neighbour, by excusing all that is excusable, by saying sincerely something good about other women, especially those who have success.

Then all the empire of respect that is given to woman, will come to corroborate the empire of truth, the reign of virtue; and woman, on her part, will fill the great end of Providence, which wishes that all power should be modest and devoted, that all influence in the creature, should serve to make the authority of the Creator respected and loved.

3rd. The apostleship of woman, as far as in religion.

Thus far, Ladies, your apostleship in the family and in the world has been rather a sweet influence than a declared mission; rather a hidden perfume, which perfumed in secret, than a flower that bloomed, attracting the gaze.

But you have in your religious mission something more positive, only this mission should not be produced excepting with great reserve; it should be an atmosphere that warms gently, and not a brazier that sparkles and crackles.

Your religious mission, first of all, is in the regularity of your example in the exercises of religion.

Examples always perfumed with charity and sweetness, and that never attract but by your goodness and your indulgence; public examples that fly egoism and the vanity of religious *exclusiveness*, that like to take part in everything, and to mingle in the common exercises; examples dictated by gratitude, rendering to religion all that it has given you, and you owe it so much! It is justice to pay it, as you do a more copious debt.

Your religious mission is a useful word, that can bring back gently those who have wandered off.

Here you will avoid two excesses: the first, that of going too fast and too violently in dealing with a husband who must be treated with great caution; the second, that of going too gently in dealing with children over whom you have authority, and for whom you are responsible.

I do not understand those extremes of boldness, there, where you should fear; and those extremes of terror, there, where nothing should make you tremble. Be careful that a husband does not repulse you with loss by that refusal, "Above all, my dear, no sermon!" It will be a proof that you went about it very badly. But on the other hand, be careful not to allow your children such an authority that you dare no longer urge them to fulfil their religious duties, that you no longer have the liberty of your table and your house on fast days, and that you tremble at all hours before the ridiculous majesty of their eighteen years.

Finally, Ladies, your religious mission is devotion to the poor and to good works; but this devotion would become an invasion, if it were not kept within wise bounds.

First of all, these works should never interfere with *works of the household*, which are yours above all else.

This outside devotion should always be approved of at home, and should be judged in the order of perfect appropriateness.

Even in these works you should avoid a too inventive spirit, too quick an imagination, the breathlessness of a panting zeal. Nothing that resembles exclusion or exclusiveness; the domination and manners of the necessary being, should not come to tarnish the gold of charity in your hand. You will remember that the holy women *followed* Jesus Christ to *serve* Him, and that it is never permitted to proceed Him, or to go in front; that in any and every case you are the daughters, never the mothers, of the Church.

Under these conditions charity calls you, not to create, not to direct and to reign, but to be docile, modest and faithful auxiliaries.

Under these conditions, charity no longer fears to tell you that it has need of you, of your ineffable words to console, of your hands, which alone nearly, know how to bandage wounds.

Go then with this mission, which God gives you; go with this triple mission of obedience in the family, gentleness in the world, devotion and reserve in religion; go, for it was by you that the world was lost; and it is by you that it will be saved, if you wish it.

FINIS.

Feast of the Immaculate Conception,
December 8th, 1894.

NOTE.

These retreats are given in the Cathedral during Holy Week. On Good Friday the subjects of the Retreat are interrupted in order to speak on the Mystery of the Passion. One of these Instructions is published in English, in pamphlet form.

www.ingramcontent.com/pod-product-compliance
Lightning Source LLC
Chambersburg PA
CBHW020754160426
43192CB00006B/329